# TIME CHART 1

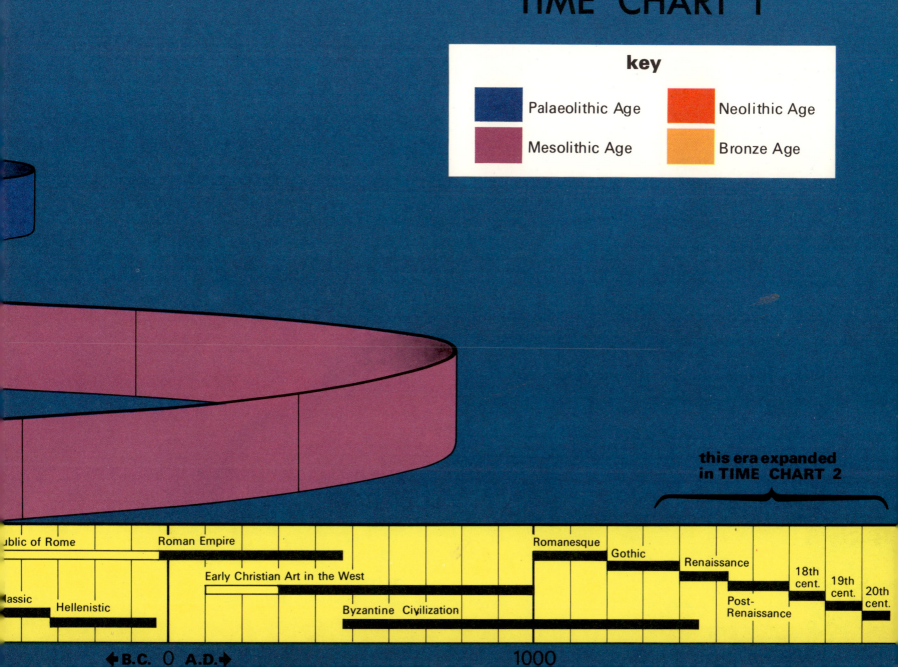

this era expanded
in TIME CHART 2

ublic of Rome

Roman Empire

Romanesque

Gothic

Renaissance

18th cent.

19th cent.

20th cent.

Early Christian Art in the West

lassic

Hellenistic

Byzantine Civilization

Post-Renaissance

◄B.C. 0 A.D.► 1000

# UNDERSTANDING ART

## THE USE OF SPACE, FORM, AND STRUCTURE

## BETTY CHURCHER

ARCA (London)

**Holmes McDougall**
30 Royal Terrace Edinburgh

Printed in Hong Kong for Rigby Ltd., Adelaide.

Published by ⱶ̦ⱱ Holmes McDougall Ltd., Edinburgh.

Copyright © 1973 by Betty Churcher.

ISBN 7157 1322–1

# ACKNOWLEDGMENTS

I am indebted to Nancy Underhill and Arthur Creedy for their invaluable assistance in the preparation of this book, and I would like to thank them for their advice and support.

Thanks are also due to all the artists who so willingly allowed their works to be reproduced, and to the following art galleries, museums, private collectors, photographers, agencies and institutions for supplying photographs and/or granting permission for their reproduction.

Advertiser Newspapers Ltd, Adelaide: 39.
Albright-Knox Art Gallery, Buffalo, N.Y.: 67, 136 (right).
Alte Pinakothek, Munich: 2 (left).
Ampliaciones y Reproducciones MAS, and Manuel Gudiol Corominas,
Barcelona: 87 (left).
*The Architect*: 31 (left).
Archives Photographiques, Paris: 73 (both upper right).
The Art Gallery of New South Wales, Sydney: 132 (left).
The Art Gallery of South Australia, Adelaide: 58, 60, 137 (right).
Ashmolean Museum, Oxford: 40 (upper right).
Australian News & Information Bureau: 105 (upper left).
Baltimore Museum of Art: 40 (lower right), 68 (right).
Biblioteca Ambrosiana, Milan: 9 (lower right).
J. Blauel, Munich: 2 (left).
Bowman Photography, Brisbane: 59, 63, 68 (centre).
The British Museum, London: 38 (right), 41 (right), 72 (both), 126 (left),
133 (left).
Marcus B. Brownrigg Studios Pty Ltd, Adelaide: 13 (left).

Canadian Department of External Affairs, and the City of Montrèal:
32 (lower right).
Cosmopress: 52, 55 (left).
Fred Douglas, Vancouver: 80.
John Edson, Melbourne: 61, 82 (upper right), 137 (left).
Fratelli Alinari S.p.A., Florence: 51, 107, 114 (left).
Gabinetto Fotografico, Florence: 42, 43, 69.
Donald Gee, Adelaide: 58, 60, 62, 137 (right).
Diedre Green, Brisbane: 34 (right).
Peggy Guggenheim Collection, Venice: 3 (left).
Haags Gemeentemuseum, The Hague: 111.
Manfred Hanisch, Essen: 28 (left and centre).
Hans Hartung, Paris: 68 (left).
Hans Hinz, Basle: 52.
Jane Hodge, Brisbane: 33 (left), 89 (right), 90 (centre).
David Holdsworth, P.N.G.: 135.
International Society for Educational Information, Inc., Tokyo: 49 (right).
Peter Jones, Melbourne: 3 (upper and lower right), 141.
John Kaldor, Sydney: 132 (left).
Peter Kelly, Adelaide: 86 (lower right), 101.
Kunsthaus, Zurich: 55 (right).
Kunstmuseum, Basle: 52, 55 (left).
David Lees: 22 (right).
Galerie Louise Leiris, Paris: 70 (upper left).
Maison Photopress, Grenoble: 54.
Mansell Collection, London: 100.
Merchant Builders Pty Ltd, Melbourne: 89 (left).
The Metropolitan Museum of Art, New York: 92.
Moderna Museet, Stockholm: 4, 78 (right), 139 (left).
Henry Moore: (3 upper and lower right), 129 (right), 141.
Ken Moorwood, Adelaide: 15, 40 (left), 104, 125.
Ron Morrison, Sydney: 5 (right), 10 (all), 11 (upper right), 17 (right), 30 (left).

Musée des Baux Arts, Grenoble: 54.
Musée du Louvre, Paris: 44 (left), 70 (right), 71, 109 (right), 115.
Musée National d'Art Moderne, Paris: 53.
Musée Rodin, Paris: 75.
Museum of Fine Arts, Boston: 138.
Museum of Modern Art, New York: 76, 77, 78 (left), 113, 130.
Museum of Primitive Art, New York: 136 (left).
National Archaelogical Museum, Athens: 126 (right).
National Gallery of Canada, Ottawa: 133 (right).
National Gallery, London: 38 (left), 45, 47 (right), 48, 49 (left), 109 (left), 117.
National Gallery, Prague: 2 (right).
The National Gallery of Victoria, Melbourne: 82 (upper left), 137 (left).
Nationalmuseum, Stockholm: 47 (left).
New South Wales Government Tourist Bureau: 1 (right).
Nezu Museum, Tokyo: 49 (right).
Roy Oorloff, Brisbane: 33 (right), 34 (left), 35 (all), 70 (lower left), 86 (both upper right), 90 (left and right), 132 (right).
Philadelphia Museum of Art: 114 (right).
Paul Popper Ltd, London: 23, 24 (all), 32 (upper right).
Queensland Art Gallery, Brisbane: 59, 63, 68 (centre).
Radio Hulton Times, London: 6 (upper right), 9 (upper right), 16, 28 (right), 95.

John and Sunday Reed, Melbourne: 61.
Reunion des Musees Nationaux, Paris: 44 (left), 53, 70 (right) ,71, 109 (right), 115.

James Robinson, Sydney: 81 (left).
Roger-Viollet, Paris: 25.
Peter Sanders, Melbourne: 9 (left), 26 (all), 87 (right), 139 (lower right), 140 (upper and lower left).
Anton Schroll & Co., Vienna: 20 (right), 21 (left).
Schwarz Gallery, Milan: 131 (left).

SCALA, Florence: 1 (left), 6 (lower right), 7 (right), 8 (lower), 19 (upper), 21 (right), 22 (left), 41 (left), 46, 55 (left), 73 (lower right), 74 (left and right), 108, 127, 128, 129 (left), 139 (upper right).
Joseph E. Seagram & Sons Inc., New York: 29.
Max Smith, Brisbane: 17 (left), 74 (centre), 86 (left), 93.
Soprintendenza alle Gallerie delle Marche, Urbino: 8 (upper), 110.
Soprintendenza alle Gallerie, Venice: 44 (right).
The South Australian Museum, Adelaide: 62.
Harry Sowden, Sydney: 12 (upper and lower right), 140 (right).
SPADEM, Paris ©: 55 (left), 70 (upper left),
R. E. Stringer, Brisbane: 11 (upper left and lower right), 12 (left), 14, 36.
Mark Strizic, Melbourne: 82 (lower left).
Sunday Mail, Brisbane: 88 (left).
Eric Sutherland, Minneapolis: 79 (right).
TAP Service, Athens: 126 (right).
The Tate Gallery, London: 50, 56, 57, 79 (left).
Andrew Taylor, Adelaide: 6 (upper and lower left), 7 (left), 19 (lower), 103 (both).

Telegraph Newspapers, Brisbane: 83 (right).
Time Inc., New York ©, and Yaffa Syndicate, Sydney: 22 (right).
Trans World Airlines, New York: 136 (left).
The Uffiizi Gallery, Florence: 42, 43.
Charles Uht, New York: 136 (left).
Union Tank Car Co., Chicago: 32 (left), 106 (both).
Vancouver Art Gallery: 80.
Hirmer Verlag, Munich: 18 (both), 20 left).
Victorian Government Tourist Bureau: 5 (left), 105 (right).
Walker Art Centre, Minneapolis: 79 (right).
Whitney Museum of American Art: 134.
A. J. Wyatt, Philadelphia. 114 (right).
John Webb, London: 50.
Yunken Freeman Architects Pty Ltd, Melbourne: 31 (right), 105 (right).

# CONTENTS

# INTRODUCTION

The aim of this book is to help you to look at a work of art and enjoy it. Of course, you can enjoy a work of art without having any real knowledge of it—by reacting spontaneously and instinctively to what you see. At the same time it is possible to know a great deal about a subject, and yet fail to get any real pleasure from it—any subject can become dry and dull if it is not enlivened by your own interest and curiosity. The greatest rewards come from a knowledge which extends, not stifles, curiosity and enjoyment.

You might ask "Why is it important to know and enjoy these things—has it anything to do with me?" The answer is "Yes, it has, because you are a person living for the most part in a man-made world." Think of the things you use each day that have been made by man.

Some of these things, such as a plastic bucket or a bathroom tap, have a practical use. Our pleasure in them comes from the efficient way in which they function. Other things add comfort to our environment, and our pleasure comes from visual gratification—for example, the colour of a table cloth, the pattern on a carpet, a colour which we choose to wear.

However, we need more than objects of utility and comfort; we also need objects which will feed our imaginations, thoughts, and curiosities. The man-made object which sets our thoughts free from the ordinary, and releases our imaginations, is what we generally term a *work of art*. A work of art cannot exist in a vacuum, its value lies in its ability to extend our awareness and satisfy the imaginative aspect of our natures. In other words, it needs *you* to make it a work of art. You could argue that many natural things we see, such as a sea-shell or the mossy bark of a tree, can work on our imaginations in the same way; however, there is an important difference. The work of art is made by a person—the artist—who can clarify the sensations and present them with such a wholeness that the experience becomes a memorable one.

By looking at what man has made in the past, and is making now, we can extend our own awareness of visual things; and this awareness must not be confined to the art gallery.

You will all be responsible in some way for the shaping of your environment. In the past, when people lived in small enclosed societies, they wore the clothes traditionally worn by that society, and built the houses that were traditionally built. Today, however, we have such a wide choice—we can choose to drive a car built in Japan or America, we can wear clothes from India, and sit on chairs made in Sweden. With so many alternatives, it is most important that we have the ability to make a wise choice.

I have divided the book into three sections, dealing with different aspects of things made by man. By making these divisions there is a danger of breaking into parts an object which is, in fact, a combination of all these things.

If you were to dissect a flower in a botany class in order to find out more about it, you should not lose sight of the radiance and sheer joy of the flower itself; in the same way, I hope the joy and radiance of art will not suffer by this analysis.

**NOTE TO THE READER**

As this book was first published in Australia, the word *we* is often used to mean *we Australians*. It was felt that the soundest way to preserve the balance of the original text, with its concrete illustrations of concepts, was by leaving well alone. It is expected that readers of all nationalities will find the information on Australian art and architecture both interesting and valuable, complementing as it does the very extensive references to European and other examples.

# SECTION ONE

# SPACE

Space is something we have experienced from the moment of birth. Our *need* for space is probably not really felt until we are deprived of it. If we were to be locked away in a small prison cell, we would then realize how important it is to have physical space in which to move freely. As well as the need for a physical space for our bodies, there is also a need for 'space' for our imaginations. If the mind is allowed no freedom, and is repressed too long, the spirit can languish like the body of a man in solitary confinement.

This section of the book will deal with many different ways in which man has used space to create the right atmosphere for our imaginations to work in.

An *architect* can arrange the inside of a building in such a way that we can feel the spirit of the building just by walking into it.

Look at these two interior spaces. In one the space suggests a feeling of awe and mystery suitable for a church—in the other, the aim is to suggest a light-hearted feeling of luxury that will make us feel extravagant and spend all our money.

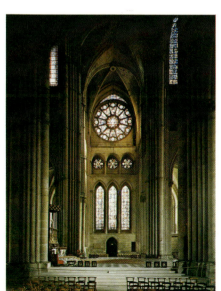

The awe and mystery of a church. This is Rheims Cathedral, the coronation church of the kings of France. 1212–1300. View looking across the transept.

A shopping centre is designed for quite a different purpose, and this can be communicated visually by its appearance. This is Roselands Shopping Centre, Sydney.

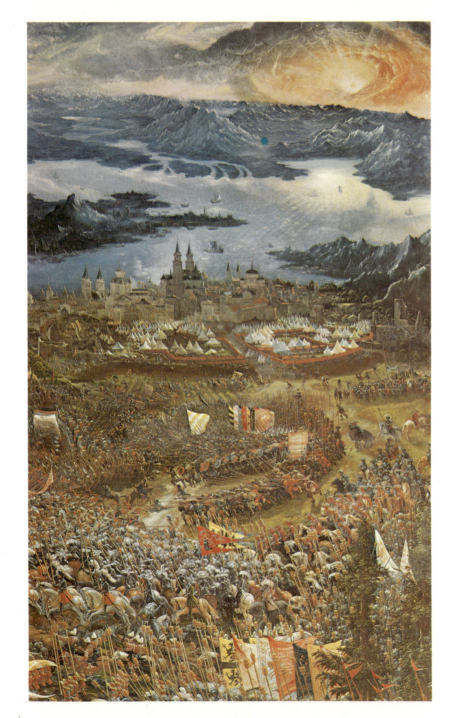

Pablo Picasso (Spanish, 1881–1973). *Still Life with Pipe*. Collage. National Gallery, Prague.

A *painter* also uses space in order to express an idea. In this painting the artist has made the canvas seem to disappear, so that our eyes and imaginations can wander off into the illusion of space that he has made for us.

Picasso has not been interested in a space going *into* the picture, but in making the shapes seem to float *in front* of the picture plane.

Albrecht Altdorfer (Bavarian, about 1480–1538). A detail from *The Battle of Alexander*, 1529. Wooden panel, 158 x 120 cms. Alte Pinakothek, Munich.

Here the artist invites us to experience the infinite dimensions of outer space or of the microscopic world.

A *sculptor* also uses space in order to give life and vitality to his work.

Henry Moore (English, *b.* 1898). *Three Rings,* 1966. Made from Rosa Aurora, 99.1 cm long. Collection: Mr. & Mrs. Gordon Bunshaft, N.Y.

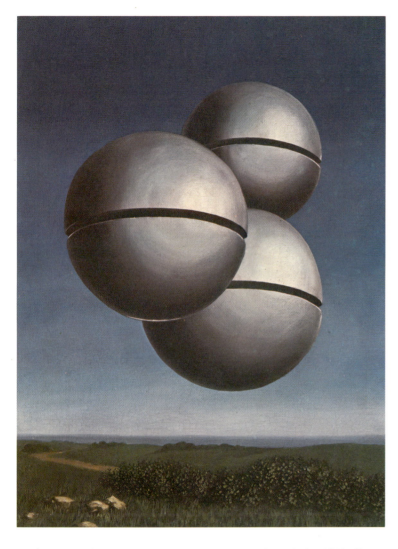

René Magritte (Belgian, 1898–1967). *Voice of the Winds,* 1932. Peggy Guggenheim Foundation, Venice.

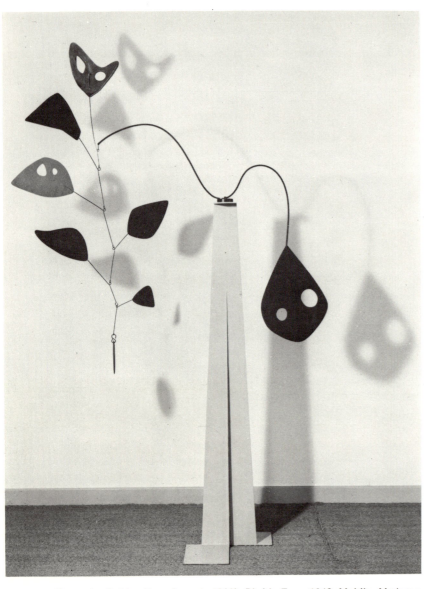

Alexander Calder (American, *b.* 1898). *Bird in Tree*, 1949. Mobile. Moderna Museet, Stockholm.

We will look first at outside spaces—the space of cities; then at the space of buildings; at the use of space in painting; and lastly at space in sculpture.

# chapter 1

# THE SPACE OF CITIES

Sociologists know that over-crowded, congested city life can cause all sorts of problems for the people living in these concentrated areas. Anyone who has pushed his way down a busy city street knows how our senses are being constantly bombarded from all sides. Physically we are jostled by other people, our eyes and ears register a multiplicity of signs and sounds. In self-defence we tend to retreat inside ourselves, to turn inwards. If our path then takes us across a park or an open space we can experience a breathing space, a relaxation. Parks and open spaces in cities are not simply a decorative addition, but an absolute necessity. The larger and more complex the city, the more important these open spaces become.

The frenzied crush and bustle of a large city can be very oppressive, and often makes us 'turn in' on ourselves.

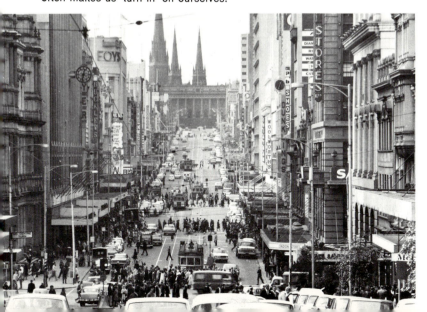

A pathway lined with trees cuts through The Domain, an oasis in the City of Sydney.

A place to meet and shop: a street scene in **Colombo**, Republic of Sri Lanka.

A place to meet and to make public decisions: the Roman Forum, reconstructed.

A place of rest and relaxation: a family picnic in the Melbourne Botanic Gardens.

A place to buy and sell: Campo dei Fiori, the large market in the centre of Rome.

Another way of relaxing in a Melbourne park: swimming after school in the pond in the Exhibition Gardens, with the Exhibition Buildings (designed in 1880 by Joseph Reed) in the background.

Man has always made use of spaces in cities, and has employed them in special ways, such as: a place to meet; a place to buy and sell; a place of rest and relaxation.

A city is a complex organism in which we are all dependent on others in order to function properly. The planning of this complex structure becomes more important as the population grows. A city could be compared to any natural organism: just like a plant it draws its nourishment from raw material and converts it to another form (the factories convert raw material into manufactured goods, the ports receive goods from the country and redistribute them to other parts of the world). This process depends on many different things taking place at the same time, and each separate part being dependent on others (e.g., the doctor needs the rubbish man and the rubbish man needs the doctor).

If the city functions well, man should be able to exist happily on his two levels—the *individual* and the *communal* aspects of his nature. Both of these aspects are extremely important to us. If a town plan ignores the individual in each of us and concerns itself only with the communal aspects of our lives, then humanity suffers. In planning a city square, for example, the planner must not lose sight of the fact that it is going to be used by individual persons, and he must try to determine what it is that individuals need from a city square. The communal aspects—city pride and status—can be equally important, but they are not all-important.

This Renaissance piazza (square) is surrounded by arcaded buildings which allow the space of the square to flow freely—the buildings define the square without blocking the space. The building you see here is Brunelleschi's Foundling Hospital, which he designed in 1419. The architect, in designing the building, had the space of the piazza in mind. The space of the arcaded walk in front of the Hospital belongs both to the building and to the piazza.

The Foundling's Hospital, on Piazza Santissima Annunziata, Florence. Designed by Filippo Brunelleschi (Italian, 1377–1446) in 1419.

Piero della Francesca (Italian, 1410/20–1492). *The Flagellation of Christ*. Signed. Panel, 59 x 81.5 cms. Urbino, Palazzo Ducale.

The facade of San Marco, Venice, showing part of the square.

Here again, Piazza San Marco (St Marks Square) in Venice is surrounded on three sides by an arcaded walk. Having entered the square through the cool, shaded arches of the arcade, one then moves into the open space of the piazza. In front are the golden domes of San Marco (St Mark's Basilica).

In both these squares there is a clearly defined, well ordered space.

You can see the same attitude in this painting by a contemporary of Brunnelleschi, Piero della Francesca. See how your eye can move freely in the perfectly logical space the painter has created. Another important aspect of the space of painting is the way the parts relate to the whole, just as they do in the Renaissance city square.

The unplanned development of the mediaeval town meant narrow and haphazard streets — this is part of old Florence.

The nineteenth century industrial sprawl: the "Black Country" around Wolverhampton, England, 1866.

A Renaissance city plan — a map of Milan by Leonardo da Vinci, which illustrates the degree of planning and order in Renaissance city development.

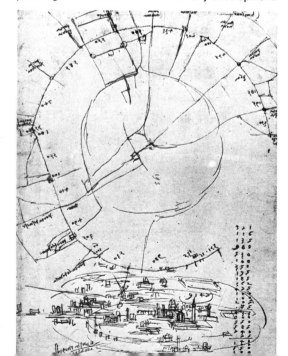

The nature of the space used in the Renaissance city square and the Renaissance painting is a reflection of the time. (The things we make reflect our thoughts and our needs.) The Renaissance era was a time of change and discovery. After the emphasis on the spiritual life and the enclosed world of mediaeval times, men's minds turned with curiosity and wonder to this world. Renaissance man consciously ordered the shape of his cities and city spaces, in contrast to the haphazard growth of mediaeval towns.

Today we have a similar need to organize our city spaces. The industrial revolution caused cities to expand rapidly. Houses for workers sprang up like mushrooms around the new centres of industry, in most cases without any thought or plan. As cities grew and spread outwards, taking up more and more of their environment, the need for imposing a plan and order to control this growth became apparent.

Freeways cut huge swathes through what might otherwise be pleasant residential areas. The automobile changes and conditions the shape of modern cities.

The modern high-rise city: this is part of Sydney.

Suburbs, suburbs, suburbs — Brisbane.

The modern city is faced with many problems. The high cost of land in city areas has resulted in the high rise building. The needs of the motor car have conditioned the structure of many modern cities. The density of city populations has created an extraordinary complexity of urban areas.

Let us take a look at city planning in our own country. Unfortunately, town planning here too often means an idea on a drawing board showing different zones and traffic routes. The new American term *civic design* suggests a more realistic approach—an artistic and social study in four dimensions. Three of these dimensions are the actual area being considered—its height, breadth, and depth —and the fourth dimension is time. Just as the seventeenth century English aristocrat planted acorns down the drive of his country estate so that his descendants could drive past an avenue of stately oaks, so the modern designer must plan for many future generations, not merely his own.

Good civic design does not rely entirely on the architecture of the city. Paris, for the most part, is composed of quite ordinary buildings—its beauty comes from its open spaces, the tree-lined boulevards, the banks of the Seine, the gardens. Australia has never lacked for space, but unfortunately we don't always see the most imaginative use of space in our civic design. There seems to be a wasteful attitude to a city's environment: to bulldoze an estate flat because it is the easiest and cheapest way to do the job; to hack back an avenue of trees, so there will be fewer leaves to rake up. The trees of Paris also shed their leaves, but the trouble of raking is considered worthwhile.

Australian cities cannot rely on the charm of ancient buildings. We do not have the works of successive generations making their contribution to the civic plan. But although we do not have the same historical heritage as European cities, we do have more space and the opportunity to do something new.

Imagine how barren this space at the corner of Eagle and Queen Streets in Brisbane would be without the Fig Tree: the designer must plan for many generations.

Kings Cross Square in Sydney, with the El Alamein Fountain designed in 1961 by Robert Woodward.

This little square by the S.G.I.O. Building in Brisbane has the same quality: it caters for human beings and therefore attracts people.

The Courtyard beside the State Government Insurance Office Building in Brisbane.

I have already mentioned that the larger the city, the greater is the need for open spaces. Large cities have a considerable population actually living in the city area itself, as well as those living in outlying suburbs. It is these people who use the parks and the squares, and it is for them that they should be designed.

This square at Kings Cross in Sydney has a very real function. It is for people and is therefore used by people. It is an exciting place to sit for half an hour, not only because of the pleasing design of a small city square, but also because it attracts life.

Photo   Planair, Edinburgh

Photo   A. L. Hunter, Edinburgh

*Above:*
Edinburgh, looking from the Meadows towards the University buildings in George Square.

*Left:*
Edinburgh University complex around George Square. The picture also shows George Heriot's School (centre) and the Castle (top right).

*Below:*
One of the teaching blocks (the David Hume Tower), viewed from George Square Gardens.

*(All photos by courtesy of Edinburgh University)*

Photo   John Dewar, Edinburgh

*Above and Right:*
Two views of the Presidential Palace in Brasilia, the new capital of Brazil.

*Below left:*
Private housing of eighteenth-century England — Royal Crescent, Bath.

*Below:*
The new Congress Hall in West Berlin.

All photos on this page from Popperfoto, London.

Do you think there is any way in which this area
could have been better used?

# chapter 2

# THE SPACE OF BUILDINGS

Now let us move from the outside to the inside—from the city square or the park to the internal space of the building itself. Different eras have produced different needs. It might be that the architect is making a house for a god, a palace for a great and powerful king, an opera house, or a private home in the suburbs. We will try to see how the space not only fits the need of the structure, but adds to the imaginative idea of the building.

First, let us imagine we are ancient Egyptians standing in the hypostyle hall of the great Temple of Ammon (Ammon means hidden god) at Karnak. We have just left the light and activity of an open courtyard, and are standing in a vast, dimly lit space, with great stone columns supporting a flat roof far above our heads. What little light there is filters down from above. It has rather the same effect as walking into a vast dimly lit forest—we feel small and insignificant and full of awe, which is exactly what the architect intended. This hall is the vestibule, or entrance, to the most secret and sacred part of the temple—the sanctuary. No one may enter the sanctuary. Behind that door, only priests and pharaohs may go. The architect has used the space and lighting of the hall to prepare us mentally, so that we can feel the greatness, power, and mystery of the god who dwells behind closed doors.

The hypostyle hall of the great Temple of Ammon at Karnak as it appears today. Built about 1312–1301 B.C. 97.6 x 48.8 metres in area, the roof was supported by 134 columns in 16 rows. In this photograph you look up the tall central columns, and can see the pierced slabs of the clerestory.

The great statue of Athena by Phidias, as she must have been when placed in the Parthenon cella on her completion in 438 B.C. In her right hand she holds a statue of Nike (Victory), and she is fully armed with helmet, spear and shield.

Now let us suppose we are ancient Greeks bringing an offering to the goddess Athena, whose statue stands in the Parthenon on the Acropolis outside Athens. As we climb the steps of the Acropolis we can see the temple standing on a stepped platform like a piece of sculpture on its pedestal. The Greek temple was not a house of worship, but a house for their god; the religious rites took place in the open, outside the temple. Thus the emphasis is not on the inside, but on the outside. The Doric columns are not just roof supports, but beautifully proportioned works of art; and the beams, walls, and pediments are carved with reliefs of such power and beauty that they have influenced the whole course of western art.

The entrance hall in this case is called the *pro-naos,* but unlike the Egyptian hypostyle hall, the area is flooded with light that shines on the white marble. It is designed to make man feel more noble, more capable of perfection, and not to make him tremble before the vast unknown. This impression of humanity is completed by the use of colour—red, blue, and gold, with natural colour on the sculptured friezes which gives a lightness to the temple in its natural setting, as well as emphasizing its beautifully appointed details.

The statue of Athena stands in the chamber behind the pro-naos (the *cella*), but she is accessible to anyone, and can be approached at any time. The great statue of Athena by Phidias (completed 438 B.C.) stood 11.9 metres high, including the pedestal, and was made from a wooden core plated with gold for the drapery and with ivory for the flesh. Forty four talents of gold (over 11 kilograms) were used at a time when the value of gold was many times its present value of about $9.60 per fine gram.

Unfortunately this statue is no longer in existence. She was standing in the cella of the Parthenon during the Roman era (the copies we have date from this period), but was last heard of in post-Roman times. She was too rich and had too much to give to survive the greed of later generations.

The cella was not merely enclosed but literally closed—the only opening was the doorway from the pro-naos. The Greeks conceived of their gods as noble and immortal extensions of the human mind and body. It was the duty of all men so to improve their minds and bodies that they could more closely resemble the perfection of the gods. The architects of the Parthenon used space, light, and colour to help men to understand this concept of their goddess—to create the right atmosphere for the imagination to work in.

Whereas the Parthenon was conceived as a shrine to house a statue, the Roman Pantheon was built as a vast enclosed space for people. When one walks into the Pantheon, one is immediately aware of the size of the great circular space above and around. Rather the same feeling one imagines a small ant might have if he were trapped inside a large, round up-turned fish bowl. The space is vast but quite static—so contained within the circular walls of the temple, and the dome above. The only opening is a circular hole, 8.2 metres in diameter, at the apex of the dome.

This opening lets in light and air, but it also let out the smoke from the sacrificial fires; for, unlike the Greek temple, this temple was designed to house the ceremony within.

An attempt to recreate the imposing space of ancient Rome can be seen in the interior of the Brisbane City Hall (opened in 1930).

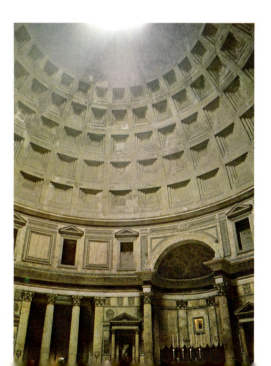

The interior of the Pantheon (the temple of all the gods), showing the great space of the vaulted dome with light flooding down from above. Built in Rome about 130 A.D., the interior remains basically unchanged.

The interior space seems to be an extension of the might and stability of Imperial Rome. Here we do not sense the spiritual mystery and unknown power of the vast, dim space of the Egyptian hypostyle hall, but rather the earthly power and pomp of the Roman state. The official Roman building seems to be a statement of authority, announcing that the Empire *is*. This is probably why Roman use of space has been 'borrowed' by so many later periods in history. If the need is to produce an atmosphere of security and strength, then men's minds seem to return with nostalgia to the space and style of ancient Rome. Each generation selects from the past that which is most useful to it. A bank likes its customers to feel that they are placing their money in a place of strength and security—that it will be kept safe for them. For this reason many banks choose to base their building design on the impressive strength of Roman architecture.

17

Hagia Sophia, Constantinople (now Istanbul). 532–537 A.D. The main dome is nearly 33 metres in diameter and rises to a height of 55 metres above the ground. This is the view looking west from the apse.

In this photograph of Hagia Sophia in Constantinople (completed 537 A.D.) we see another vast and imposing interior space, like the Pantheon, but this time we do not get the same feeling of enclosure.

Let us imagine we are standing on the floor under the great central dome. We would immediately want to explore, to walk past the marble columns of the arcades you see to the left and right of the central space, to find the stairs that lead up to the gallery directly above these arcades. The space is centred under the

The south-west gallery of Hagia Sophia, looking towards the northeast wall. The name *Hagia Sophia* means *Divine Wisdom* (not Saint Sophia).

main dome, but moves out in a complex series of smaller spaces, rather as if a centrifugal force had thrown them out from the centre. Unlike the Pantheon, we cannot stand in the middle and see it all.

The enclosure of these spaces—the walls, domes, and half domes —are given an illusion of fragility by the use of shining, luminous-coloured marble up to the level of the gallery; and the entire surface above is faced with mosaic tiles of gold and many colours. In this way the solid nature of the brick 'case' which encloses the interior space is disguised by the shine and colour of the surface, so that the domes seem to float above us without any visible means of support.

In order to understand why the nature of the space used in buildings changed in the 300 years that separate the Pantheon and Hagia Sophia, we must try to understand the spirit behind this later building. It was one of the first great Christian cathedrals to be built. Christianity was declared the official religion of the Roman Empire by the Edict of Milan in 327 A.D., during the time of the Emperor Constantine. Constantine had divided the Roman Empire so that there could be two centres—Constantinople in the east, and Rome in the west. (Later, in 402 A.D., Rome was abandoned as the western capital, which was moved to Ravenna, further north on the other side of the Italian peninsula.) Constantine had seen that the empire, like the unwieldy dinosaur, was growing too large for a single nerve centre. He built the first official Christian church in his new centre, Constantinople. This church was later destroyed by fire, and the Emperor Justinian decided to build a great new cathedral dedicated to the glory of God. A contemporary historian recorded his impression on first walking into the cathedral: "It seemed as if the vault of heaven was suspended over one."

Here we have another cathedral, but once again the space has changed. Instead of the circular area of Hagia Sophia, with its spaces bubbling upwards and outwards from the centre, we have an immensely tall and narrow space, which invites us to walk forwards to the high altar at the far end. It is rather like walking up an avenue of tall and slender trees, whose branches meet lightly over our heads. The rhythm of movement as we pass the vertical columns, the repetition of the spaces between the columns, makes a measured beat as we move through the space. This is the Gothic cathedral of Bourges in France. It was begun in 1192 and was finally completed in 1275. As 655 years separate the completion of Hagia Sophia and the beginning of Bourges Cathedral, we must consider what had happened in Europe during the intervening years.

The year 1000 A.D. was prophesied to be a fateful year—a year of total catastrophe. To the people of Europe, this was just another anxiety to add to the troubled times that had existed ever since the fall of Rome. (The western Roman Empire had collapsed by 476 A.D.—the eastern Roman Empire, however, had continued under the leadership of a series of powerful emperors. You will remember that Justinian built Hagia Sophia in 537 A.D.) Barbarian invasions in western Europe had disrupted the established order of the country—there seemed little hope for the future. However, when the millennium year came and went without the expected fire and brimstone, Europe seemed to heave a great sigh of relief, and the reprieve from heaven produced a hopeful spirit which expressed its

Bourges Cathedral, France. 1190–1275. Looking down the nave towards the apse.

Do you notice any similarity between this avenue of trees and the nave of a Gothic church?

19

deliverance in the building of many new churches to the glory of a merciful God.

There was an upsurge in faith, new religious orders were founded, and the church took on a new authority. It became the controlling and organizing power in place of the crumbled Roman state. By this time the barbarian invaders had become part of mediaeval society, and were making their contribution to the culture of Europe.

Bourges Cathedral is the final triumphant stage of a gradual development which started with the first Christian churches to be built in the west. Looking back to these early Christian churches we will see how the architects developed the interior space to fit the growing needs of the church.

This church is an ancestor of Bourges Cathedral. It is Sant'Apollinare in Classe, at the little town of Classe, which was the port for Ravenna in Justinian's time. Here the space is contained by the flat roof above. The movement of the interior is from door to high altar and apse at the back, not upwards and outwards as in the interior of Hagia Sophia. Sant'Apollinare in Classe was consecrated in 549 A.D., just twelve years after Hagia Sophia, but was built in the style adopted by the western countries for their early Christian churches. Hagia Sophia became the pattern for Christian churches in the east.

The style of Sant'Apollinare is ideally suited to the Christian ritual. A large number of people can stand in the long central nave and look towards the high altar where mass is being said. The arcades that separate the nave from the two side aisles seem to lead the eye forward to the altar by the rhythmical movement of the arches.

Why then would men need to make changes? Why alter a shape if it so fits the requirements of the building?

Perhaps the answer lies in the growing importance and status of the church itself. You will remember the new spirit of hope that followed the year 1000 A.D., and that this extended the power of

Sant'Apollinare in Classe. 534–549 A.D. An early Christian basilican church. Above the arches is a band of portraits of the bishops of Ravenna (Apollinarus was the first bishop of Ravenna), and the mosaics in the apse show the saint preaching to his flock.

The cave-like nature of Romanesque space is demonstrated by this photograph of the crypt of Tornus Cathedral.

Tournus Cathedral, built about 1009 A.D., in the French province of Burgundy. This view of an aisle shows the great solid walls and columns, the semi-circular vaults: the dark mystery of the Romanesque church.

is not the weightless space of Hagia Sophia, but the mysterious space of caves and caverns. The house of God becomes an impenetrable fortress.

By the twelfth century, the power of the church, which had been expressed in the massive structures of Romanesque architecture, had extended this vision even further to become a vision of an awe-inspiring structure that would turn men's minds at once to the might of God. By this time, mediaeval architects had worked out a more efficient means of extending the interior space upwards. The heavy semicircular vaults of Romanesque times became the pointed vaults of Gothic architecture. We will deal with the structural aspects of this change in the next section, but first I want you to compare the interior space of Bourges with that of Tournus.

In Bourges the space seems to lose all sense of gravity, and soar effortlessly upwards. The walls and columns look almost too fragile to support any real weight from above. A space shaped quite differently from the Hagia Sophia, but quite as awe-inspiring and breathtaking. It is interesting to watch people as they walk into a Gothic cathedral, and to see how the interior space affects them. Regardless of religious beliefs, automatically voices are lowered to a whisper, and even the noisiest tourist tip-toes reverently in the

the church. This new strength and authority of the church gave birth to a new style, Romanesque, which better suited the aspirations and spiritual intensity of the time.

Blunt, massive, and overwhelmingly strong, the new space moves up into great stone vaults, supported on sturdy stone piers. This

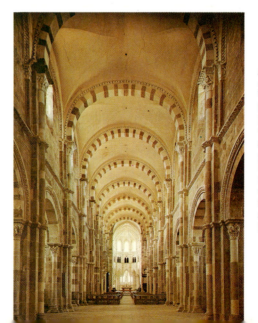

Another Romanesque church: S. Madeleine, Vézelay, also in Burgundy. 1089–1206. However, although the vaulting of the nave is still rounded, there is a greater feeling of lightness and upward movement; this building of a later date is starting to show some of the signs of the development into the Gothic style.

21

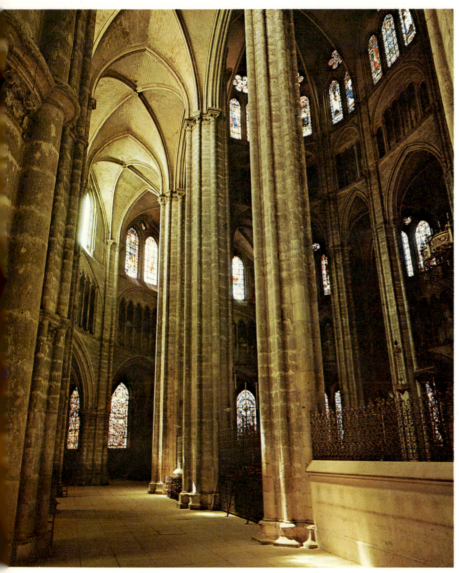

spiritual atmosphere of the cathedral. To stand in a Gothic cathedral when the choir is singing, and the tall narrow space of the nave is filled with sound, is a most moving experience. The acoustics of the interior space are perfect for the religious ritual. The architects, sculptors, and stained glass artists who worked together to produce the Gothic cathedral were giving a visible and tangible form to the religious feelings of the time. By enriching the cathedral, they were glorifying God.

In this photograph of Bourges Cathedral we see again the vertical, slender height of the interior. Columns, arcades, windows, and vaults seem to grow from a single irresistible impulse. As the great trees of a rain forest move up to the light, so these columns seem to be trying to stretch up to reach heaven itself. Have another look at the church interior illustrated on page 1. That is Rheims Cathedral, another of the great Gothic cathedrals of France.

This is a photograph of the opening of the Second Ecumenical Council in the nave of San Pietro (St Peters Cathedral) in Rome. It is interesting to see the interior being used, to see how the shape has been designed for the function—the religious ritual.

Bourges Cathedral again: this view down one of the side aisles, looking towards the east end, shows the height and upward movement of Gothic cathedrals.

The logic and practicality of Renaissance space is illustrated in this scene of the opening of the Second Ecumenical Council in St Peters, Rome. Built over a period of 120 years between 1506 and 1626, under many different architects.

By 1506 Bramante had drawn up the first plans for this great cathedral, just seventy nine years after the completion of Rheims Cathedral in France. Look back to the photographs of the interiors of Rheims and Bourges, and compare them with the interior of St Peter's. Probably the first thing you will notice is that the tall, narrow space of the Gothic cathedral has become the majestic barrel vault of the nave of St Peter's. If you were to compare the feeling of St Peter's space with the spatial feeling of any period we have already considered, would you have chosen the interior of the Pantheon?

The space of the Pantheon is grand, imposing, and *logical*—a practical, clearly defined, well lit interior. The interior of St Peter's has some of these qualities. When we discussed the Renaissance square and the Renaissance painting (the Piero della Francesca *Flagellation*), we noticed this same attitude to space—a space you could understand and move freely in.

The fact that Renaissance space abandoned the religious mystery of Gothic times and looked back to ancient Rome for inspiration suggests that other changes were also taking place—changes in the way of life and thinking of the time. If you look at a map of the Mediterranean you will see that the peninsula of Italy is centrally placed. It would be the obvious place to receive the riches of the East pouring into Constantinople by trade routes from China, India, Syria, etc., and then to redistribute these goods to the rest of Europe. For this reason Italy gradually became a wealthy trading centre. By the fourteenth century, cities such as Venice and Florence were thriving and prosperous—Shakespeare gives us a picture of this in his *Merchant of Venice*. Now, in order to conduct a business of this trading nature there is a need for a well educated class of people who can act as company lawyers, foreign diplomats, efficient book-keepers, and company executives. Universities flourished and scholars began to search the libraries for earlier works to build on.

In the writings of ancient Rome they found a society that was also concerned with law, organization, and economics. The excite- ment of rediscovery soon spread, and scholars, philosophers, and artists were soon eagerly searching for the grandeur that was Rome. There was a spirit of re-birth (the word *Renaissance* means *re-birth:* it was coined by a French historian, Michelet, in 1855). This spirit of discovery led to a desire to find out more about man and the world he lives in. Of course the church was still a most important influence in their lives, but now there was a new enthusiasm for the down-to-earth reality of this world. Look again at the interior of St Peter's. What you see there is actually the combined work of several architects. Bramante drew up the first plans, they were then worked on by the painter Raphael, and later again by the sculptor-painter-architect Michelangelo. At the end of the barrel vault you will notice that the space seems to open out—this is the space under the vast dome which was designed by Michelangelo. This controlled use of space devised by the Renaissance architects established a pattern in European architecture.

It was the engineers of the nineteenth century who gave the lead to the next really significant use of architectural space. Cast iron, and later steel, became the new building material: a material of strength and versatility, which ideally suited the function of new engineering structures. The web-like system of metal girders which roofs this railway station is spanning an area far greater than any stone vaulted roof could attempt.

Inside Victoria Station, London. 1859–1866. Robert J. Hood, Engineer. The potentialities of iron were used and advanced by the nineteenth century engineers in many railway stations.

The engineers and architects soon realized the possibilities of cast iron being used as an exciting new visual experience in architecture. One of the earliest experiments of this nature was made in the Crystal Palace, which was built for the Great Exhibition in London. It was opened by Queen Victoria in 1851, and was the first vast glass and cast iron building (it covered an area of 7.3 hectares).

The Crystal Palace, built to house the first ever International Exhibition in 1851, was designed by a horticulturist, Sir Joseph Paxton (English, 1803–1865), as a giant conservatory. Destroyed by fire in 1936. It was 564.5 metres long, and because it was constructed of prefabricated iron and glass parts, took only 10 months to build.

When Gustave Eiffel built his Eiffel Tower for the Paris Exhibition of 1889, he produced one of the first great steel structures. When one is climbing the spiral stairway, the tower becomes a 'space cage'. The feeling of vertigo is due not only to the height above ground but to the fact that one is suspended in an unenclosed space devoid of horizontals and verticals.

Gustave Eiffel's (French, 1832–1923) Tower, more than 300 metres high, demonstrates the tensile strength of steel. The view looking up into the structure illustrates the spatial uncertainty of a space without horizontals and verticals. Built in 1889 of structural steel, it was the tallest building ever erected until after the First World War.

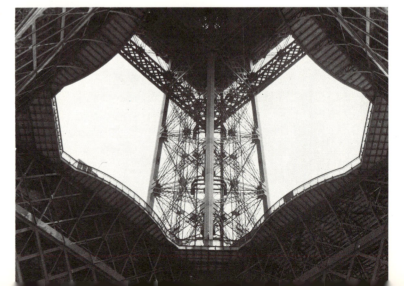

Machinery Hall, designed by two Frenchmen: architect Dutert and engineer Contamin, for the Paris International Exhibition of 1889, it was built of steel and glass, was over 400 metres long and nearly 46 metres high.

Machinery Hall was also built for the Paris Exhibition of 1889, and had the widest span yet built—the steel girders spanned 116 metres.

The railway station, the Crystal Palace, and Machinery Hall are concerned with the functional enclosure of space, while the Eiffel Tower is concerned with the functional possibilities of steel; they all led the way to a new concept of building, in which new materials and advanced technology gave rise to the exciting developments of this century.

We have been discussing how architects in the past have used space to give meaning and reality to the nature and need of their building. In discussing the use of space in modern architecture we must start by trying to decide what are our modern needs. We will deal with modern church architecture, and will see how modern concepts and technology create a space to express twentieth century attitudes towards religion. But there are also other needs: the need to solve the problems of congested living and limited ground space; the need to construct large communal structures—office blocks, administrative buildings, stadiums, shopping complexes; the need to provide people with a domestic space in which to live—an interior which will give the security of enclosure and the benefits of new developments in the use of space.

This century has evolved an entirely new attitude to the imaginative use of space. Science has made us aware of the infinite nature of outer space, and of microscopic space. It is as if we stand somewhere in the middle of an indefinable space which extends to infinity on each side. No longer can we restrict ourselves to the comforting confinement of Renaissance space. (In that era man's knowledge was, for the most part, confined to that which could be experienced—the tactile, measurable space of this world.) It would be surprising if this new knowledge and awareness did not affect the forms and shapes man makes now.

It would serve no purpose to have a dream of constructing a free-flowing unrestricted space without having the technology to execute it. However, the technical and scientific needs of this century have developed the use of many new building materials.

One of the world's biggest buildings, which encloses 3 679 000 cubic metres of space, is the Vehicle Assembly Building, part of the Apollo Space Programme installation at Cape Kennedy, Florida, U.S.A. It is so vast that clouds and rain have been known to form *inside* it. Even more extraordinary is the fact that the launching tower is mobile. A crawler tractor, 39.7 metres by 43.9 metres, lifts the structure with assembled rocket and slides it to the launching point at a rate of 1.6 kilometres per hour. The technology required to perform this feat (it would be the same as picking up the Eiffel Tower and transporting it) is also the technology which has enabled modern architects to explore new possibilities of space and structure.

The discussion on the modern use of space will deal with some examples of religious architecture, with the large communal structures of this century, and lastly with domestic architecture.

25

The pilgrims chapel of Notre Dame du Haut near Ronchamp in France. Designed by Le Corbusier (Swiss, 1887–1965), and built 1950–1955 of thick reinforced concrete.

In these photographs we see a number of different views of the chapel of Notre Dame du Haut, near Ronchamp in France, designed by Le Corbusier. If you look first at the ground plan you will notice that he has totally abandoned the traditional idea of a building (an enclosed rectangle, cube, or circle). The walls curve around areas, defining interior space, but the outside can flow in, and the inside out. The three crosses mark three small chapels, each with its own tower to admit light from above. The dotted line marks the concrete slab on which the building stands.

If you look back at the exterior views of the chapel you will notice that Le Corbusier has tried to give his building a feeling of simple honesty—that it has been made by a person for people to

Two other exterior views of Le Corbusier's Notre Dame du Haut. Note the slits on the towers, which admit light into the chapels, and the sculptural quality of the water spout (which feeds into an underground cistern.

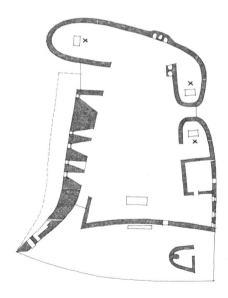

use; the feeling that it has grown naturally to fill a need. Le Corbusier was impressed by the beauty and dignity of small Mediterranean fishing villages. The houses seem to grow out of their environment, their shape being determined by the immediate needs of the men who built them.

However, the concept of this chapel is totally twentieth century. The interior space is comparatively small, the main nave is only a little more than twelve metres wide, but since the space is not cubic—the ceiling slopes up and the walls curve out—we have no feeling of being in a small, confined area.

The irregular, unexpected interior space is further enhanced and made more alive by the unusual lighting. As well as the light which comes from apertures in the three towers, the main nave is lit by irregularly placed openings. These openings are narrow in the outside thickness of the wall (and are fitted with very beautiful stained glass), but open out like a funnel to become larger inside.

STAINED GLASS

A cross-section of the walls, showing the funnel-like window openings, and the hollow 'shell' walls.

Light seeps into the cool intimate atmosphere of peace and prayer. When you compare this modern chapel with earlier churches, you can understand how religious needs have changed.

We feel that here is not so much a statement of the awe inspiring might of God, as a statement of man's need for contemplation and prayer.

In Notre Dame du Haut we can notice an important aspect of twentieth century thought: a desire to present a total experience as one single image. We experience the Gothic cathedral as we move from one part to the next, many parts making up the whole image. We could explain these different processes of arriving at a total image with this diagram, where, in the second part, we do not gradually arrive at 10, it is part of the structure.

Here is the interior of a church, recently built in Germany, which was designed by Professor Gottfried Bohm. The shape and lighting of the interior space gives a modern version of the mystery of religious thought. Notice that it is built of concrete and that the space moves forward and back, rather like the shapes of an abstract painting. It seems that either the interior space is pushing up into the space outside the building, or the outside is pushing down into the interior space.

The larger communal buildings of this century make full use of new building materials, modern engineering, and technology. As well as the functional use of these new building materials, they are also used imaginatively. The glass front of the I.C.I. Building on

The vaulted ceiling of Professor Bohm's Pilgrim's Chapel reaches to a height of 34.8 metres above ground.

The fan vaulting of the Gothic cloisters at Gloucester Cathedral. Can you notice any similarity between this Gothic vaulting and the modern vaulting used by Gottfried Bohm in his Pilgrim's Chapel?

Pilgrim's Chapel, Neviges, Germany. Designed by Professor Gottfried Bohm. Built in 1968 of reinforced concrete poured against boards.

28

Circular Quay in Sydney reflects the sky and drifting clouds. The facade becomes a moving picture of sky and harbour—part of the life of the building's environment. The reinforced piers which support the building at the entrance to Australia Square (page 12) impart a feeling of lightness to the massive concrete structure.

The rectangular, steel framed, glass covered towers of Mies van der Rohe have been one of the strongest influences on multi-storey buildings. Unfortunately, they have been copied so often in such an unimaginative, insensitive way, that the boredom of looking at

The Seagram Building on Park Avenue in New York City. Designed by Mies van der Rohe (German, 1886–1969), and completed in 1958, it has 42 storeys and is curtain-walled with bronze panels and tinted glass.

ugly city blocks makes it hard for us to see van der Rohe's originals with a fresh eye.

In 1954 the Seagram whisky firm had plans drawn up for a new office building on Park Avenue, New York City. The site occupies half a midtown Manhattan block. A characteristic of a modern office building is that it is designed for nobody in particular—tenants come and go, each with different needs for the use of the inside space. Van der Rohe's building has a core of lifts, stairs, telephones, electricity outlets, etc., but is without fixed internal walls. The tenant can partition his area to suit himself.

Seagram & Sons wanted to occupy part of the building themselves, the rest to be let to tenants. You can see that van der Rohe has provided a large area of rentable space on a comparatively small ground area. He has used the greatest economy of materials, giving the building an elegance and a lightness by the extensive use of glass.

Joern Utzon, a Danish architect, won an international competition for the design of the Sydney Opera House in 1957. The requirements in this case are very different from those of the Seagram Building. The need here is to house the stage and auditorium of the Opera House on one level, and rehearsal and dressing rooms on a lower level. The building is situated on a spit jutting into the harbour in the middle of the city. It can easily be seen from all sides: from the ferries and boats of the harbour, from the bridge, and from the air as planes come into Sydney airport. As it is a building to be seen very much 'in the round', Utzon has focused attention on the roof. When one thinks of space in relation to this building, one thinks not so much of the interior space, but the way the building occupies the space of its environment. For the same reason the architects of the Parthenon concentrated on the outside of the building, embellishing it with sculpture and colour. The concrete sails, which are faced with white ceramic tiles, take on a sculptural quality as they push upwards and outwards into the blue space of the harbour. The building seems to float on the water, its giant white sails seen against the small white sails of the harbour boats.

Perhaps the reason that this building has been so criticized is that it is a poetic concept, and this age seems to find difficulty in making room for the poetic. It has been criticized for the length of the building time; yet some Gothic cathedrals took centuries. It has been criticized for the amount of money involved; but think of the cost of an F-111 fighter bomber!

The Sydney Opera House, designed by Joern Utzon (Danish, *b.* 1918): the pre-cast concrete shells faced with white ceramic tiles rise to a height of 67.4 metres. Building commenced in 1959, and was completed in 1973.

The T.W.A. Terminal Building at Kennedy International Airport, New York, designed by Eero Saarinen (Finnish, 1910–1961), built 1956–61 of reinforced concrete.

Eero Saarinen, who designed this terminal building at the Kennedy International Airport in New York, also considered the space around his building. He was one of the adjudicators who selected Utzon's design as the winning entry for the Sydney Opera House Competition. The free-flowing concrete structure has so little apparent gravity, one wouldn't be altogether surprised to see it take off with the aircraft! By not enclosing a rigid rectangular space, Saarinen has designed a structure with the streamlined elegance of a jet plane, the very shape of which gives us an expectancy of flight.

The Federal German Pavilion at Montreal's Expo 67. Designed by Professor Frei Otto (German, *b.* 1925), using steel cable net and PVC-coated polyester fabric.

The Sidney Myer Music Bowl, in the Kings Domain, Melbourne. 1959. Architects: Yunken, Freeman Brothers, Griffiths & Simpson (now Yunken Freeman Architects Pty Ltd). The canopy protects the stage and a large audience in addition to acting very successfully as an acoustic bowl.

This great plastic tent was designed by Professor Frei Otto as the pavilion for West Germany at Montreal's Expo 67.

It is an interesting answer to the problem of roofing really large areas, such as exhibition pavilions, shielding areas of parks, swimming pools, transportation centres, or shopping complexes. By using plastic as a membrane suspended from a steel net, Frei Otto is making use of a new building material. The light steel cable net is swung from eight masts, with the plastic membrane suspended about 30 cm below it on hundreds of hangers. A polyester fabric with a tough PVC (polyvinyl chloride) coating is used, which is permanent and durable, but many times lighter than any other building material.

Buckminster Fuller also explores the possibilities of enclosing vast areas of space with the least and lightest amount of material. He even envisages being able to enclose large areas of cities to make them not only weather proof, but pollution proof. Fuller's geodesic domes work on the geometry of energy (push and pull energy). The interior space of a Gothic cathedral is maintained by a balance of tension between the weight of stone in the vaults pushing down and out, and the mass of stone in the walls and buttresses pushing up. (You will understand this more clearly when we have dealt with the section on structure.) Fuller's domes maintain a balance between the internal volume of air and the external volume of air. Metallurgy and alloy chemistry have given him a material capable of withstanding enormous tension, so that he can span areas unthought of in earlier times.

In fact, the larger the dome becomes, the more efficient is the geodesic structure. As the interior space volume increases, so the internal pressure of air increases (the enclosed air heats more rapidly than the outside air, causing it to become lighter and so equalize the pressure). Fuller's preoccupation with enclosing the maximum volume with the minimum of material led him to produce structures so light that they could be air-lifted into position by helicopter. He designed a series of small geodesic domes made of

A recent photograph of the Wood River Building, a geodesic dome designed by Buckminster Fuller (American, *b.* 1895).

The Indian adobe pueblo (village) of Taos, in New Mexico, U.S.A., has been built of sun-dried mud, with additions made over many centuries all being versions of the same single form-type. Unity yet variety.

polyester fibreglass to house radar equipment for the DEW line (Defence Early Warning). A line of these radar domes, known as Ra-domes, stretches across northern America. Similar domes are also used by the Marine Corp as rapid shelters. They can be heli-lifted into position ahead of the advancing marines.

It was in 1927 that Fuller first conceived the idea of mass-produced air delivery structures—but he had to wait nearly fifty years to see his dream become a reality.

Before leaving the large communal structures of this century and dealing with domestic architecture, we will look at this housing complex which falls into both categories. It was designed by Moshe Safdie as part of Montreal's Expo 67 *Man in the Community* project. Safdie offers this as a solution to high density living. He feels that cities cannot continue to support the spread of low density suburban areas. At the same time he feels that the thirty-storey apartment building with its tiny fenced balconies is not the answer.

From a distance, Habitat looks like an entire village clinging to a hillside; in fact it is a total environment of houses, shopping

facilities, streets, car parks, and pedestrian roadways. The houses are pre-cast factory-made concrete units arranged in such a way that space flows in and around the structure, giving each unit sun, air, and an uninterrupted view of the harbour. Each house has its own garden, built on the roof of the unit below, and each opens onto a pedestrian roadway. In this way Safdie has tried to provide the benefits of suburbia: privacy, an individual identity, a garden, fresh air, and sunlight, but assembled together into a restricted area.

Habitat is proving very successful: everyone who lives in this housing complex designed by Moshe Safdie (Canadian, *b.* Israel 1938) finds it a very pleasant and rewarding environment.

The standard Australian suburban allotment: Is there any more privacy and individuality here than in Safdie's Habitat?

Safdie has said that to build economically is a moral obligation of our time. He is not referring only to the economic use of space, but to the economic use of *all* the world's resources.

## Space in Australian Domestic Architecture

Domestic space must provide an enclosure for living which functions for the special needs of the individuals who are going to use that space; and which also functions for the special climatic situation in which the house is to exist. In Australia we have many wonderful climatic advantages—long periods of fine weather, prolific tropical or sub-tropical vegetation; and several climatic disadvantages—hot and humid periods, and heavy rains at certain times. In designing a house, an architect tries to make the most of one, and, where possible, overcome the inconvenience of the other.

Architecture in Australia has a wonderful and unique heritage in the old timber structures of the early settlements. These were built from the most readily available building material—wood.

The simple functional structures have an impressive dignity and honesty, although the men who built them had no intention of building an interesting and pleasing structure, but were simply using the available materials in the most logical and functional way and overcoming a limitation in building materials—they had no nails, bolts, or prepared timber to work with.

The early settlers built their own slab huts with similar ingenuity. The walls were constructed of slabs, split from logs by means of mauls or wedges; the roof was covered with sheets of stringy bark tied to rafters of sapling poles. The roof rafters were secured to the walls by wooden pins, as nails were too scarce and too expensive to be used by the average settler. If a fireplace was included, it occupied one end of the hut, and this end was often built of sundried bricks or of galvanized iron in order to minimize the risk of a fire in a wooden structure.

A slab hut at Laidley, Queensland. Note that the roof is made from wooden shingles, which were widely used as a roofing material before the advent of galvanized iron.

Over the years the building of slab huts was considerably refined. There were wooden floors, plastered inside walls, make-shift ceilings of either calico or sailcloth nailed between the ceiling joists. (These ceilings had an unfortunate tendency to collapse without warning under the weight of accumulated birds' and possums' nests!)

Verandahs were fairly universal as they provided a cool and shady place to sit or to store perishable food. These settlers' homesteads were often built with excellent workmanship—with frames dovetailed and wedged into rigidity without the aid of a single nail. Usually the timber of these buildings was left unpainted and allowed to weather to a natural and pleasing silver-grey, which harmonized with the grey-greens and golds of the Australian bush.

Early Queensland houses were lifted about 50 centimetres clear of the ground on timber stumps—this allowed better ventilation below the floor; and by placing tin caps between the stump and the house, the constant threat of white ants was minimized. By the 1880s Queensland houses were being raised on tree trunk stilts 2–2.5 metres high. In a generally hot climate subject to heavy downpours of rain, the 'underneath the house' became extremely useful for laundries, storage areas, etc. As with the earlier slab huts, the verandah became increasingly a living area—a place to sit and talk, a place to eat, even to sleep in hot weather. To protect the verandah from the sun, screens of open slats or trellis work were often fixed between the posts—these provided shade, and at the same time allowed the free passage of cooling air.

In order to make use of the air in the roof space as a heat insulator, the roof was generally steep and fairly high. Gabled ventilators built into the apex of hipped roofs allowed the hot air to escape, as well as producing the interesting silhouette shape of the early galvanized iron roofs. For this reason, rooms were arranged in a square—so that they could be covered by a tall pyramid roof, topped with a ventilator (the pyramid roof has no pockets in which hot air can be trapped).

This domestic structure of a box of rooms surrounded by verandahs and raised on stilts had grown naturally out of the existing

A typical raised Queensland house, in Indooroopilly, Brisbane. The height above ground not only helps cool the house by better ventilation below the floor, but is also the best answer to the depredations of white ants. Note the ventilator in the apex of the roof.

Note the intricate decoration on this house in Ipswich, and also the exposed timber framework, arranged in a decorative pattern.

The charm of this old house in Rosewood, Queensland, lies in the hand-worked decoration. In spite of its dilapidated state we can still see the pride and care that went into the finishing of every detail. Because these details relied on the skill and imagination of an individual, and have not been stamped out by a machine, they have the simple charm and quality of all successful folk art.

In a hot climate, trellis on the verandah affords extra protection from the sun; and also closes out the external environment from the house.

The fashion which developed in wooden suburban houses in Queensland in the 1930s and 1940s widened the gap between the internal space and the outside. Without the space of the wide verandahs, the house became a closed-in wooden box on stilts.

This is what can happen when the demands of the environment are ignored. Although perhaps a logical development of the trellised verandah, there is now no sheltered place for people to sit and relax outside, and no means of protecting the walls of the house from the direct heat of the sun.

climatic conditions and available building materials. Many examples are not only distinctive and indigenous, but also extremely elegant and comfortable to live in. There was ample scope for easy decoration by an imaginative carpenter. The brackets of verandah posts, gables, verandah rails, etc. became features which gave rise to a type of folk architectural decoration.

We have discussed the many practical advantages of these early Australian houses, noticing how the shape evolved to meet local conditions. However, in almost every case there is a tendency to cut off the outside as much as possible. Many of these houses seem to 'turn in' as if the immediate environment is a hostile one which must be shut out at all costs. Notice how the house in this photograph presents a closed face to the external world; there is no attempt to let the outside in or the inside out.

For a time, city dwellers, bent on fashionable status houses, tended to ignore the early tradition of Australian domestic architecture and, along with the neat wooden boxes there appeared, in the suburbs, Spanish villas, Tudor houses, English brick bungalows, etc. These borrowed shapes had all evolved for conditions in other places and at other times, and therefore they fail to make full use of the existing local environment and climate.

Today's designers realize that our environment is not necessarily a hostile one which must be ignored or shut out, and are allowing outside spaces in, and opening inside spaces out. Because the origins of the early Australian timber house had been in rural homesteads where gardens and vegetation were difficult, if not impossible, it is understandable that those settlers should want to set themselves apart from a dry and barren environment. However, in the cities of Australia we have the possibility of a particularly lush and prolific growth of trees and shrubs. This, together with a favourable climate, creates ideal conditions for utilizing outside areas as an extension of living space.

The verandahs of the old houses provided for an 'outside' protected space, but with the disappearance of the verandah it became necessary for modern architects to find some alternative in open, but protected, living areas.

Many modern Australian architects are again making use of wood as a building material, as can be seen in this photograph of the Vice Chancellor's residence at the University of Queensland designed by Brisbane architect John Dalton. Notice how the interior space is not fixed or enclosed, but moves freely from one part to the next, yet each part maintaining its own character and intimacy. This fluidity of interior space did not exist in many of the old timber structures; however the cheapness of building materials made it possible for the early houses to have a generosity of interior space (large rooms and high ceilings), which would be impossible now. Architects today are forced to work with more confined spaces, yet a sensitive use of these more restricted areas can produce a sensation of a generous and expansive interior.

The vice-Chancellor's Residence at the University of Queensland, designed by Brisbane architect John Dalton. An example of a fluid interior space, with a spacious feeling despite the economical area.

# chapter 3

# SPACE IN PAINTING

In dealing with the space of paintings, as opposed to the space of buildings, we have a very different problem to consider; for in this case the space does not really exist. All paintings are in fact quite flat, but the artist can create an illusion of limitless space if it suits his need: if the idea he is expressing needs that sort of space.

In this chapter we will start by discussing the two main types of picture space: 1, the space that seems to go in *behind the surface,* a three dimensional space; and 2, the space that moves *across the surface,* a two dimensional space. To illustrate this I will select two paintings from different times and cultures in order to see not only how the space has been used, but also why the artist has used this particular type of space as a means of expression.

Having looked at these two typical examples, we will then go back to Roman times and see how and why men have used pictorial space at different times in history.

## Three Dimensional Space in Pictures

You will remember that the scholars and artists of the Renaissance became interested in the possible scope of man's talents and abili-

ties, and also in the nature of the world in which man lives. We have seen this interest expressed in the well ordered space of the city square, and again in the illusion of a well ordered space in *The Flagellation of Christ* by Piero della Francesca. As there was a general interest in the physical nature of the world and in the possibilities of people's minds, it is not surprising that artists also should become interested in making their paintings a mirror image of the real world. The painting becomes a stage, but whereas the theatre belongs to a moment in time, and then is gone forever, the painting can resist time and 'freezes' its moment forever.

We can see this very clearly in the picture by the Flemish artist Jan van Eyck. This is painted in oil on a wooden panel 81.8 cm high, and shows the marriage of an Italian merchant and his wife. It was intended to serve as a legal document with the artist acting as witness to the marriage: on the wall above the mirror is written "Jan van Eyck was here 1434".

Van Eyck has made the surface of the wooden panel seem to melt into a sensation of real space, so that we can see, with his eyes, every detail of the room lit by the clear sharp northern light coming through the window. Like the Piero della Francesca, the space is logical and easy to understand. Pretend you are walking

Jan van Eyck (Flemish, 1385–1441). *The Marriage of Jan Arnolfini and His Wife*, 1434. Oil and tempera on a wooden panel, 82 x 59.5 cms. London, The National Gallery.

into the room, go up and look in the mirror, then across to sit on the bed—it all seems possible, doesn't it?

The mirror on the wall behind reflects the room so that we see the same space in reverse, with the reflection of two people not in the picture (the two witnesses to the marriage needed by law) standing in a doorway which opens into another space. This gives a feeling of infinite recession, like those wonderful Chinese carved ivories of a box within a box, within a box, etc.

## Two Dimensional Space in Pictures

The making of an illusion of space that does not really exist has not been the aim of all artists. The ancient Egyptian artist who painted this picture of a scene from a banquet is telling his story in a different way. He is not interested in making a physical space for our imaginations to move in. He does not particularly want to record the scene as it would have appeared to us, had we been there at the time. Instead he has used line, shape, and colour to make the whole experience live; not merely to convey just how it *looked*, but to suggest the sound of the music and the rhythm of the dance. Look at the four figures on the left (the singers and the woman playing the flute). See how the lines of their dresses and

*Girl Musicians Singing and Dancing at a Banquet.* Egyptian, eighteenth dynasty *(c.* 1600 B.C.–*c.* 1350 B.C.). Fresco from the Tomb of Nacht. London, British Museum.

the tiny plaits of their hair form a vibrating rhythm, like the plaintive notes of the flute. Look now at the dancers. Can you visualize the rhythm and movement of the dance?

You may well be wondering what all this has to do with space. Although the artist has not used a space going into the painting (a three dimensional space), he has used two dimensional space. See how the space *between* the figures has been used. He has given the dancers room to move, and without this space our minds could not easily reconstruct the rhythm of the dance. The horizontal lines of the Egyptian hieroglyphic writing which occupies the space between the singers and the dancers serves as a link between the two.

If the painting loses something by not showing us the space of the banqueting hall in which the dance took place, it certainly gains something by its direct approach. Notice how the scene is placed right before our eyes, so that all the action takes place on the surface of the wall, with no part disappearing into a hazy distance (rather like our seeing a stage show from the front row of the stalls).

In order to understand why there was this desire for closeness and clarity, we must understand why the picture was painted.

This is one of the paintings from the tomb wall of a high court official. The Egyptians believed that the soul of the dead man would need his earthly possessions in his after-life. For this reason his body was carefully and skilfully mummified so that the soul could re-inhabit the body after death. By surrounding the dead man with colourful and pleasurable scenes of things that had delighted him on earth, the tomb lost something of its cold finality, and gave the Egyptians hope that they could relive these pleasures in the next life. In these tomb paintings we see scenes of hunting, harvest, grape gathering, wine making—all the comforting everyday activities. In this sense they appear almost as an inventory of worldly life, but far more real than any written inventory; hence the desire for clarity.

This photograph of people dancing demonstrates how inselective the camera can be, and how it freezes action.

If you compare this photograph of people dancing with the Egyptian painting, you will notice that the camera, because it cannot select and arrange, freezes the action. Notice too, how the complication of superimposed shapes reduces the impact of the scene.

As a general rule, artists use this two dimensional space, which projects the image towards us, at times when the desire is to communicate an idea clearly; when the artist wishes to impress the image of the picture without the distraction of unimportant details which could cloud the idea.

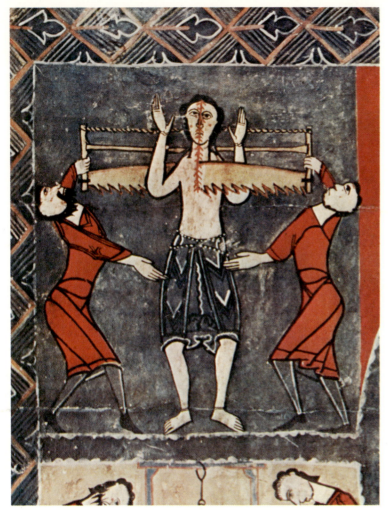

*The Martyrdom of St Juliet, c.* 1100 A.D. Frontal of the Church of Saints Quirico and Juliet, Spain. Barcelona, Museum of Catalan Art.

*Two Daughters of Akhnaton.* Egyptian, eighteenth dynasty. Fresco. Ashmolean Museum, Oxford.

Henri Matisse (French, 1869–1954). *Pink Nude*, 1935. The Baltimore Museum of Art, Cone Collection.

Although over three thousand years separate these three works, you can notice a similar use of space. In each case the flat areas of colour seem to move towards you so that the image is firmly impressed upon your mind.

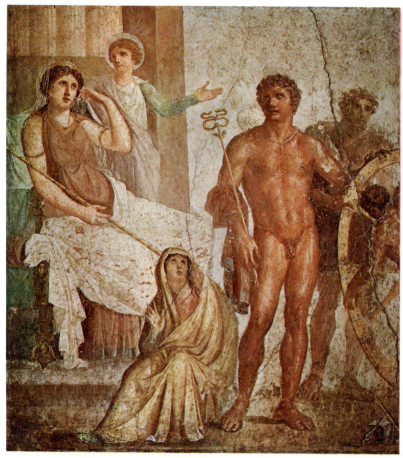

*Ixion Tied to a Wheel in the Presence of Juno*, first century A.D. Fresco from the Casa dei Vettii (the house of the Vetti family), Pompeii. About 122 cms high.

## Space in Pictures from Roman Times to the Twentieth Century

This painting is on a wall of a private house in Pompeii, which was a prosperous seaport of the Roman Empire. The volcanic ash which buried Pompeii for nearly 2000 years protected the city so well that we are still able to see the large, airy, beautifully decorated villas almost as if they were new.

The rooms of these houses faced inwards to an open central courtyard. As most of the light came through the doors opening onto this court, there were few windows, and this left large areas of unbroken wall space for decoration. Look again at the painting reproduced here: is this the space that goes into a picture such as van Eyck used thirteen centuries later when he painted *The Marriage of Jan Arnolfini and His Wife?* Or is it a two dimensional space that seems to push the shapes towards you, as we have seen in the Egyptian wall painting? The artist has painted a space going *in,* and so convincingly that the wall seems to open up, making the room appear much bigger than it really is. Remember that the person who painted this picture belonged to the same culture as the person who designed the Pantheon. In both painting and building the space seems to be the result of clear and logical thinking.

You will remember that after the fall of the Roman Empire, it was the Christian church that became powerful enough to provide something of the unity and order that Europe had enjoyed under the rule of Rome. It was the church that commissioned the artists of the time to provide pictures that would not only decorate the church itself, but would also instruct the congregation—by surrounding them with images of the holy family and saints.

This portrait of a young boy was painted by an artist in the Roman province of Egypt in the second century A.D. These paintings replaced the carved heads of the much earlier mummy cases.

Roman portrait on a mummy case from the Imperial Roman province of Egypt. Second century A.D. London, British Museum.

41

Notice how real and alive the face looks, how the artist has used shadow to make the nose seem to come forward. One would expect that this tradition of Roman painting would be adapted to depict the religious figures in the churches, but in fact, this was not the case.

In the early days of Christianity, the Eastern church founded by Constantine in the old city of Byzantium (renamed Constantinople), quickly became powerful and influential. (Remember that in the sixth century A.D. Justinian built the great church of Hagia Sophia.) The officials of this Eastern church were so anxious to stamp out all traces of paganism and the worship of idols, that for a time they banned the use of any images at all in their churches. However, they later relaxed this rule to allow certain religious symbols to be used, as long as the symbols could not be confused in people's minds with the actual thing.

Therefore the reality of Roman painting would not serve the purpose of the church, and artists directed their energies towards making signs for religious figures that would have a direct impact and immediately communicate the religious message without the confusion of physical reality. These Byzantine symbols soon became the traditional and accepted way of representing the religious story, and quickly spread through Italy, via Venice and Ravenna, to influence church art in Europe for many centuries. The Spanish Romanesque fresco on page 40 is an example of this religious style.

The picture on the left was painted by the Italian artist Duccio on a large wooden panel just over 4.5 metres high. It was painted in the last years of the thirteenth century, and still shows the influence of Byzantine symbolism and use of space. You will notice that Duccio has not carried on the Roman tradition of 'fooling the eye' with an illusion of space that seems to go behind the surface of the painting, instead he is using space in a way similar to that of the ancient Egyptian artists.

Duccio di Buoninsegna (Italian, *c.* 1255/60–*c.* 1315/18). *The Madonna Enthroned*. Painted in 1285 for the Rucellai Chapel in the Church of Santa Maria Novella, and so is often called the *Rucellai Madonna*. Panel, 450 x 290 cms. Florence, The Uffizi.

Giotto (Italian, 1266/7–1337). *The Madonna Enthroned.* Painted about 1310 for the high altar of the Church of the Ognissanti (All Saints). Panel, 325 x 204 cms. Florence, The Uffizi.

The gold background is quite flat, and clearly defines the objects in the painting. The Madonna is seen as a flat shape that seems to float weightlessly in front of the throne. The gold edging of her gown becomes a line full of energy and life which climbs its way up from the hem until it finally circles her face like another halo. Duccio's aim was to present his idea in such a way that the Italians of the thirteenth century would understand immediately that he was portraying the divine nature of the Virgin Mary. For this reason he used traditional signs (the haloes, the gestures, the gold background symbolizing the light of heaven, the colour of the Virgin's robe symbolizing purity, even that energetic gold line which symbolizes the life of the Spirit). To the people of that time, these signs would be as easily understood as road signs are to us today.

The other picture of the same subject was painted by Giotto only twenty five years after Duccio painted his picture. In this painting the angels seem to be standing in the space around the throne, and the Virgin has the weight of a real person sitting on her throne. You will notice that Giotto is using some of the same traditional signs (the arrangement of the figures and the haloes); he also wanted to communicate with people, but this time our minds can wander from the religious message. We may start looking at the faces of the angels and Virgin as people, and start thinking of their human aspect—Duccio will not allow us to do that, and keeps us firmly to the religious point.

This picture by Giotto is one of the first signs of the new attitude which marks the Renaissance era. The forceful and beautiful sign language of earlier Christian art gives way to an interest in recapturing the experience of vision. It is as if this new era picked up the thread of Roman painting and, with new knowledge and skills, extended all the possibilities of three dimensional painting. We have already seen the degree of real space that van Eyck managed to achieve in his *The Marriage of Jan Arnolfini and His Wife* over a hundred years later.

Leonardo da Vinci (Italian, 1452–1519). *Mona Lisa*, also known as *La Gioconda* — a play on the name of the lady (she was married to a Florentine official Francesco del Giocondo) and the Italian word *giocondo*, meaning cheerful, joyous. About 1500–1504. Oil and tempera on wooden panel, 77 x 53 cms. Paris, The Louvre.

Notice how the dark shape of the head separates from the lighter tones of the background; how the soft shadows of the face seem to mould the features with such reality that our fingers can feel the contour of rounded cheek and jaw line. If you let your eye move slowly across the surface of this painting from one side to the other, it is almost impossible to believe that the strokes of paint that make Mona Lisa's head, sit right beside the strokes of paint that depict the rocky cliffs of the background. In spite of this illusion of reality, *Mona Lisa* is still a dream, and seems always to be just beyond our grasp (the distant space is very much a dream space, unlike the space of Jan Arnolfini's bedroom, which one can imagine actually moving about in).

What has happened to the space of this picture? Do you notice that the calm serenity of *Mona Lisa* has gone, and the space of

Jacopo Tintoretto (Italian, 1518–1594). *The Body of St Mark Being Transported*. Painted sometime after 1568. Oil on canvas, 421 x 306 cms. Venice, Accademia.

Leonardo da Vinci was fifty one years old when he painted this portrait in oil on a wooden panel 0.76 metres high. It was painted seventy years after van Eyck's picture, and, like van Eyck, Leonardo da Vinci has made the surface of the panel seem to disappear; but this time as we look through the window of the frame, we look into a world of Leonardo's own creation. It is as if the panel becomes a mirror reflecting in its surface the vision of the woman and the landscape behind her. As with a mirror, the painting has a flat surface, with the image seeming to form behind it.

44

El Greco (name really Domenikos
Theotocopoulos; Greek, 1541–1614).
*The Cleansing of the Temple,*
1584–94. London, The National
Gallery.

the painting seems to rush you in dramatically along that white line on the paved court; at the same time the figures in the foreground are bursting out of the canvas towards you. It is rather like being caught in a whirlpool of violent movement.

Tintoretto, a Venetian artist, painted the picture, which shows the body of St Mark being removed for burial on sacred ground, some fifty years after Leonardo painted *Mona Lisa;* he gives the story a feeling of high drama by the turbulent movement of the space and the figures in the space. Instead of sitting back behind the frame like Mona Lisa, the action seems to be surging forward and around you as in theatre-in-the-round.

The space in this painting is restricted by the wall at the back which runs parallel to the picture plane. The movement and gestures of the crowd seem almost too violent to be contained within the narrow, claustrophobic space. If you block out the one place where the space opens up (the archway behind Christ's head), you can feel this close confinement even more, and realize how important this release is. The picture shows the Saviour driving the money changers from the temple, and was painted by El Greco, a Greek painter who settled in Spain about the year 1577. When El Greco left his homeland of Crete, he went first to Venice where he worked for a time in the studios of Titian.

45

This painted ceiling in the church of Sant'Ignazio (St Ignatius) in Rome extends even further the dramatic space of El Greco and of Tintoretto.

The space fools our eye so cleverly that it is difficult to see where the real architecture of the church stops and the painted architecture takes over. The vaulted ceiling seems to open up to giddy heights until we are looking into heaven itself.

Andrea Pozzo (Italian, 1642–1709). *St Ignatius Carried into Paradise*, 1691–94. Fresco, 30.5 m long. Church of Sant'Ignazio, Rome.

46

When you first look at this picture by the Dutch painter Rembrandt, you see the saint reading by the light of a window; but you may not realize the importance of the space that surrounds the figure. Rembrandt's space is not the obvious space of the ceiling painting in St Ignatius. In order to realize the importance of Rembrandt's space I want you to try an experiment: focus your attention on the figure of the saint and stare hard at him for some time. If you are patient enough, and look for long enough, you should slowly become conscious of the size of the space around the man. The space seems to expand until you feel that man is a small and vulnerable thing in relation to the vast spaces that surround him. This experiment should help you to understand how important it is to give paintings a little time. The quick glance that takes in the subject matter only is not enough.

Here we have quite a different sensation of space; this is the more comforting confined space of your own room, filled with light and air that moves around all the objects of the room. This picture was painted by Vermeer, another Dutch painter who was working in Holland at the same time as Rembrandt.

Rembrandt van Rijn (Dutch, 1606–1669). *St Anastasius.* Signed and dated 1631. Oil on wood, 60 x 48 cms. Nationalmuseum, Stockholm.

Jan Vermeer van Delft (Dutch, 1632–1675). *Lady Standing at the Virginals.* London, The National Gallery.

Meindert Hobbema
(Dutch, 1638–1709).
*The Avenue at Middleharnis*, 1689.
London, The National Gallery.

Have you noticed that although artists have used landscape as a setting for figures, no one has yet painted a landscape for the joy of the landscape itself? It was the Dutch painters of the seventeenth century who first turned their attention towards the poetry and beauty of landscape as a thing to be seen in its own right.

How far from the religious dogma of Duccio's painting is this Dutch landscape by Hobbema. Nearly 400 years separate it and Duccio's *Madonna Enthroned*. See how Hobbema has used light to sharpen the sensation of space and reality: look for a while at the tree trunks and feel this sensation of space which Hobbema evokes by the use of light. Notice the way the yellow of the man's coat is placed in the narrow space made by the avenue of trees. Compare this yellow with the pink of the distant church spire—the yellow, because of its greater energy and intensity, comes forward, setting up a three dimensional space relationship with the buildings behind. Now focus your attention on the birds in the sky, feeling them move in a limitless space.

48

John Constable (English, 1776–1837). *The Hay Wain*, 1821. London, The National Gallery.

*Evening Light on a Fishing Village.* Thirteenth–fourteenth century. Chinese hand scroll painting, attributed to Mu-Hsi. Tokyo, Nezu Museum.

Like Hobbema's landscape, this picture by the English painter John Constable is concerned with the landscape; the figures are only incidental. To the English of the nineteenth century this painting was hard to understand; it was reviled as being 'unnaturally green'. As a rule, people react violently to any change in thought or tradition; it is much more comforting and less exacting to follow habit or custom.

It is hard for us now to understand how the sparkle of light and the fresh greenness of a Constable landscape could ever upset anyone. (It will probably be equally hard for the people of the twenty first century to understand the outraged feelings caused by Picasso's paintings in the early years of this century.)

Compare this Chinese hand scroll painting with Constable's *Hay Wain* and Hobbema's *Avenue*. All three are landscape paintings, the Chinese one being much earlier than the two European examples. In order to look at the Chinese painting properly, you must look at it as the artist intended. This painting is a hand scroll and so was never intended to be seen at one glance as it can be in the way it is reproduced here. If you could hold the scroll in your hands and gradually unfold the picture, the experience of the landscape would be quite different. Place two pieces of paper across the picture reproduced here, leaving a gap of about 2.5 cm between them. The paper should cover the reproduction, only exposing 2.5 cm of the picture at a time. Now move both pieces slowly across, starting from the right hand side. See how the picture starts on the shore, with the mist hanging low over the trees; as we move on we come to the water's edge, the mist thickens and a mountain top floats mysteriously above the lake; further on we find ourselves in the middle of the lake in a space which has no boundaries. The water and sky merge together and the small fishing boat seems to float in space. As we move on, the mountains of the other shore start closing in, the houses of the village on the far bank are just visible through the mist, and finally we reach the firm comfort of the rock and trees of the left hand side of the picture. When you were in the middle of the lake, did you feel the enormous nature of endless space (a space, like infinity, that has no limits)? The Chinese artist who painted this picture in the mid-thirteenth century is asking you to come and *feel how he felt* as evening closed in over the lake. Constable is asking you to come and look and wonder, to *see what he saw* when the sun sparkled on trees and water.

Joseph Mallord William Turner
(English, 1775–1851). *Snow Storm:
Steam Boat off a Harbour's Mouth
making signals in shallow water and
going by the lead. The author was
in this storm on the night the Ariel
left Harwich,* 1842. Oil on canvas,
91.5 x 122 cms. The Tate Gallery,
London.

This oil painting, by the English artist Turner, was exhibited at the Royal Academy in London in 1842. It shows a small boat caught in a violent snow storm in the English channel. See how the boat seems to be caught in the spiralling whirlpool movement of sea and sky. The mast of the boat is caught in a tunnel of space that looks like the eye of a cyclone. (Have you seen a photograph of the cloud movement of a cyclone taken from a satellite?) One of the interesting things about this painting is the way the space seems to be all around you; we noticed Tintoretto using this space that moves forwards as well as back in his painting of *The Body of St Mark being Transported.*

Turner was so concerned with translating a real experience to his canvas that he had himself lashed to the mast of the steamboat *Ariel* during such a storm. He wrote: "I was lashed for four hours, and I did not expect to escape, but I felt bound to record it if I did." Critics described the painting as 'soapsuds and whitewash', to which Turner replied "What would they have? I wonder what they think the sea's like? I wish they'd been in it."

This painting is obviously not a concocted idea of a storm at sea, but is the result of Turner's trying to communicate his experience—you can see the very brush strokes taking on the fury of the storm.

50

## The Twentieth Century Revolution

All the painters we have looked at from Giotto to Turner have been concerned with using a three dimensional space to give shape to their ideas. Now, for the first time since the Renaissance era, artists of the twentieth century have become interested in the *surface* of the picture again. This does not necessarily mean that they have stopped using any space that goes into the picture, but that there is a more obvious tension between the colours on the surface and the colours that seem to move back in space.

One of the earliest signs of this dual space that keeps the eye interested in the surface as well as in the 'inside' space can be seen in this portrait by the French painter Paul Cézanne, who painted it in 1899, just at the turn of the century.

Can you notice the two kinds of space at work simultaneously? Cézanne has structured his vision by re-building the forms he sees before him with planes of colour. He directs our eye over each surface by controlling the energy of colour—for example, a surface which curves away from the eye is built with planes of colour which decrease in energy as they move back in space. It is as if he were modelling with colour energy instead of light and dark. However, as well as this sensation of space which moves our eye over and around each shape and into the picture, there is also a surface vitality which creates pulls and tensions across the surface of the canvas. Notice that no section of the painting falls away into a negative dark area—our eye can scan across the picture, conscious of the undeniable existence of the surface while at the same time registering forward and back movements into an illusionary space. The lines which hold the major areas together (see page 114) add to our experience of the picture plane.

Cézanne gives equal acknowledgment to the factual experience of vision and to the intrinsic nature of a painting—that it is a flat sheet of canvas activated by lines and colours. He structures his vision into an architecture of tautly related parts (somewhat like a breathtakingly complex house of cards in which each new card

Paul Cézanne (French, 1839–1906). *Portrait of Ambroise Vollard*, 1899. (Vollard was a Parisian art dealer and collector, who encouraged many painters. He arranged the first exhibitions of work by Cezanne, Picasso and Matisse, among others.)

must be placed absolutely in accordance with the previous ones; each addition making the structure more tense and precarious, but also more exciting). It was this aspect of Cézanne's work which excited Picasso and Braque nearly ten years later, when they were making their first experiments into Analytical Cubism.

Pablo Picasso (Spanish, 1881–1973). *The Bull-Fight Fan* (Spanish title: *L'Aficionado*), 1912. Oil, 136 x 82 cms. Basle, Kunstmuseum.

When we first look into this picture by Picasso, we see a complicated structure of shapes that move forward and back within the limits of a very narrow space; almost as if we were looking at a carved relief.

Picasso once remarked: "I paint objects as I *think* them, not as I *see* them." His aim is reality, but not the reality of vision that moves evenly over a form. Try looking at a person, not with a vague glance that takes in the whole figure, but look intently at parts. You may look first at the point of the elbow, then let the eye move to the angle of the wrist, to the cylinder of the neck. Now close your eyes and try to visualize these points of reference in space. Look again at Picasso's painting. He has looked in this way at a bullfight fan sitting at a café table with his newspaper *Le Torero* and a carafe of wine.

Picasso has not been interested in the perspective view of reality that the camera gives, instead he is interested in the way his eye selects a vertical shadow on the man's hat, which continues down into the form of the face, which in turn relates other verticals and diagonals picked up by his eye. By fragmenting the shapes he sees into facets of closely related planes, he orders his vision to the essential shapes of the cylinder and the cube. In this way shapes take on a new structural geometry inspired by his vision, but ordered by his mind.

Notice the way the moustache seems to float across the strong architectural forms of the face, underlining the fact that it is a superficial attachment. The sharp pick of the banderilla appears in the centre of the picture (the banderilla forms a diagonal direction as it leans against the edge of the table). At the end of the man's fork are the letters *T O R*, a fragment of the word *toro* (a bull)—the man is eating steak, perhaps the bull that died in the ring. Picasso uses words in this picture to suggest associations (he took great interest in the fights at Nîmes), but also, being flat, the words draw attention to the flat surface of the picture.

Between the years of 1907 and 1914 Picasso and his friend Georges Braque were involved with this new attitude to vision and painting.

Renaissance perspective was concerned with the reality of vision from one fixed viewpoint—a particular event viewed from a particular point in space. Picasso felt that this reality was not the only reality. What we *see* when we look at a cup from the side is not necessarily all that we *know* about the cup; its circular base, its internal space, the circle of the lip, are not apparent from this side view. Therefore, he introduced a multiple viewpoint in order to incorporate the many aspects of an object—not just to describe each object from all sides by a sequence of haphazard 'views', but more to show those aspects which reveal the fundamental, essential nature of the objects.

In the painting by Picasso reproduced here, the many planes or surfaces which make up the complicated vision of a man sitting at a café table are no longer forced to obey the laws which set them in their logical place according to logical space, but are allowed to float forward or back according to the needs of the painting, or the needs of the concept or idea (which was as real to Picasso as the visual impact).

These paintings of Piscasso and Braque belong to their *Cubist* period—so called because their interest in this new structure of planes caused a critic to remark of Braque ". . . he despises form, and reduces everything—houses, landscape, figures—to geometrical designs, to cubes."

In this still life, Georges Braque suggests the space volume of the room by means of flat planes of colour arranged without perspective. The intensity and weight of these planes of colour determine the distance of objects from the eye as well as their distance from one another. This picture was painted in 1942, during the years of the second world war; and something of the mood of the war and of Paris during the Occupation is evident in the stark shapes of this still life, stripped bare of any decoration or ornament.

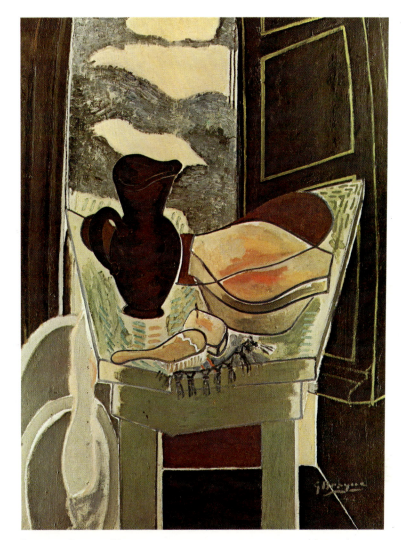

Georges Braque (French, 1882–1963). *In Front of the Window*, 1942. Paris, Musée d'Arte Moderne.

Notice the way Braque uses line instead of *chiaroscuro* (shading) in order to invest each shape with its own particular life, volume, or energy.

Matisse is controlling the space of this picture with colour, he wants the reds of the Spanish rug on the wall and the reds on the bench to be as active and alive as possible. He therefore does not dull the reds of the background in order to make them recede into the picture. He is more concerned with a true sensation of colour than with the illusion of space.

Henri Matisse (French, 1869–1954).
*Still Life with Red Carpet*, 1906.
Musée de Peinture et de Sculpture,
Grenoble.

54

Paul Klee (Swiss, 1879–
1940). *Little Picture of a
Pine Tree*, 1922. Basle,
Kunstmuseum.

Alberto Giacometti (Swiss, 1901–1966). *Head of a Woman*, 1952. Oil on
canvas, 73 x 60 cms. Zurich, Kunsthaus.

This *Little Pine Tree* by Paul Klee stands in its own magical
space—but it is not a space that can be measured out or logically
understood. We react to it in an intuitive way, realizing that this
is not a particular space being described. (Klee tried to avoid
what he calls "the deadly finality of fixation".)

In the midst of this space which is full of surprises and the unexpected, the little tree stands confident and sure of its existence.
Around the tree, the world forms itself into enclosing boxes; boxes
which imprison each part, holding each part to its own particular
nature; but the tree, drawn by the warm energy of the sun, is the
only form whose limits have not been defined, is in the process of
becoming.

The woman in this portrait by the Swiss artist Alberto Giacometti seems to be compressed by the space around her. It almost
seems as if she started off much bigger, but gradually became compressed as the space moved down. Giacometti's sculpture also has
this feeling of tension between gravity pushing *down* and the life
force of the form pushing up and out.

55

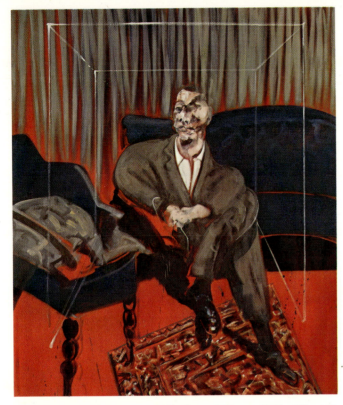

Francis Bacon (English, *b.* 1909). *Seated Figure*, 1961. 165 x 142 cms. The Tate Gallery, London.

This painting by the British artist Francis Bacon has something of the same 'space-pressure' as the Giacometti portrait. Notice how the white 'cage' traps the figure in the space of the room, making the space tangible in spite of the flat sensation of the carpet. Bacon has painted the inanimate objects—the floor, the chairs, the curtain behind—as static objects in space. However, the man, because he has the properties of life and movement, seems to be shifting slightly as we look at him. The white line, which spells out the space around the man, moves into the figure and loops around the crossed leg, giving the form a feeling of space and movement, as if he has just this minute crossed his legs.

Roy Lichtenstein, an American painter, is interested in the transformation which occurs when an ordinary 'everyday' image becomes greatly enlarged. His painting, *Whaam,* is very large, it has the proportions of a road hoarding, but is seen from close quarters on the gallery wall, and so has a powerful physical impact. Unfortunately, when the painting is reproduced in a book, it becomes so reduced in size, that it returns to its source—the comic strip, and so loses much of its impact.

Lichtenstein uses flat colours, so the images are very frontal (as in an Egyptian frieze painting). However, in spite of this flatness there is a three dimensional space implied by the warm mauve shadow on the aeroplane which floats forward from the cool mauve background, and also by the precise perspective drawing of the aeroplane.

Lichtenstein chose the cartoon as it has no previous connections with a 'work of art'. It was a new-born subject, free of any history of expressive interpretation, and yet it is very much a part of modern man's imagery. Of these paintings he said " . . . once I've established what the subject matter is going to be, I'm not interested in that . . . I think of it as an abstract painting when I do it. Half the time they're upside down anyway, when I work."

He was once asked why he selected this particular subject matter, and in reply told a story about his small son's embarrassment at school by his father's then abstract paintings. Lichtenstein drew a large Mickey Mouse for his son to prove to his schoolmates that Daddy could in fact draw! It was this drawing he says, that made him realize the universal nature of the cartoon image, an image which is as immediately recognizable to modern man as a religious icon would have been to mediaeval man.

Of course, these paintings caused some concern when they first appeared on the walls of an art gallery, because they upset the set concept of the 'gallery-goer' as to what constituted a work of art.

Roy Lichtenstein (American, *b.* 1923). *Whaam*, 1963. Magna on two canvas panels, 17.3 x 40.7 metres. The Tate Gallery, London.

Lichtenstein and other American painters of the 1960s became interested in creating a new imagery which bore some relevance to the urban, modern life they knew. It seemed pointless to paint a picture of a cow standing under a tree when their world was one of cement pavements, skyscrapers, neon signs, and processed foods. Their new imagery was drawn from these aspects of modern life, as well as from the cinema, television, advertizing and, in Lichtenstein's case, the comic strip.

Because they chose popular everyday aspects of modern life, they became known as *Pop Artists*. Just as Constable made people more aware of the quality of the English landscape, so these American Pop artists make us more aware of the quality of their environment—the American city. If we live in a city anywhere in the world, these same things are very much part of our life, and must be looked at and considered, rather than blindly accepted or disregarded.

## Space in Australian Painting

For many years Australian painters were concerned with recording the particular nature of Australian landscape. For this reason we do not see the same interest that European painters had in the space structure of a picture.

Tom Roberts painted this landscape just eight years before Cézanne painted his *Portrait of Ambroise Vollard*. However, it resembles more the space of a Constable landscape. The subject of course is different and depicts the Australian scene, with the choking red dust raised by the stampeding sheep, and the crow flying low over the paddock.

Tom Roberts (Australian, *b.* England, 1856–1931). *The Breakaway*, 1891. Oil on canvas, 134.6 x 165.1 cms. Adelaide, The Art Gallery of South Australia.

Here are three Australian paintings, all painted in the years between 1941 and 1951. As you can see from these three reproductions, the artists are still very concerned with the distinctive nature of the Australian landscape. In Russell Drysdale's *Man Feeding His Dogs* we feel the vast, untamed, and inhospitable land of the interior, on which trees and people seem to balance precariously.

Russell Drysdale (Australian, b. 1912). *Man Feeding His Dogs*, 1941. Oil on canvas, 45.8 x 61 cms. Brisbane, Queensland Art Gallery.

59

Arthur Boyd (Australian, *b.* 1920).
*Cyanide Tanks, Bendigo,* 1950.
Tempera on masonite, 79.4 x 121
cms. Adelaide, The Art Gallery of
South Australia.

In Arthur Boyd's *Cyanide Tanks, Bendigo,* the crows fly, dogs bark, and men labour in a landscape of dry red earth, grey slag heaps of disused gold mines, and the soft grey-green of Australia's grasslands.

Sidney Nolan's *Ned Kelly* rides across a sparse, anonymous scrub land where the few dry trees punctuate the space. Kelly has been depicted as a sign, so that he moves mysteriously across the space, half real and half unreal. The empty mask symbolizes the myth of Kelly, which has outgrown the man.

If you compare the work of these Australian artists with the work of their European contemporaries, you can see that they have been more concerned with a literary idea—the nature of Australia and the Australian story—than with the nature of space and form in the picture itself.

Sidney Nolan
(Australian, *b.* 1917).
*Ned Kelly*, 1946–47.
Ripolin on masonite,
91.5 x 122 cms. In the
possession of Mrs
Sunday Reed,
Melbourne.

61

The aboriginal bark painting comes from Arnhem Land. Probably the first thing you notice about this picture is the vitality of the line. There is no illusion of space or volume, but your eye, moving across the surface, follows the movement of the root as it pushes its way through the earth. Notice how the energy of the plant is directed downwards; the life force of the plant takes place beneath the surface; and all this is told by the expressive use of the line itself. That line, that is the root, pushes down, folds in on itself, meets an obstacle, almost peters out, but gathers force and moves on. To the aboriginal artist, every mark he makes, each line and dot, has absolute symbolic meaning, at no time is he aimlessly space filling with decorative strokes. This urgency of expression creates the dynamic tension and life of the painting (we saw this same intensity of meaning in the paintings of ancient Egypt). Even paintings that may appear to us as abstract designs of circles and cross-hatched lines are in fact graphic descriptions of actual things. The circles may be waterholes; the water which feeds these holes, the bands of cross-hatching; parts where white predominates indicating fresh water while yellow corresponds to dirty stagnant water.

Aboriginal Bark Painting from Arnhem Land. *An Underground Tuber and Its Vines.* Ochres on bark. Adelaide, The South Australian Museum.

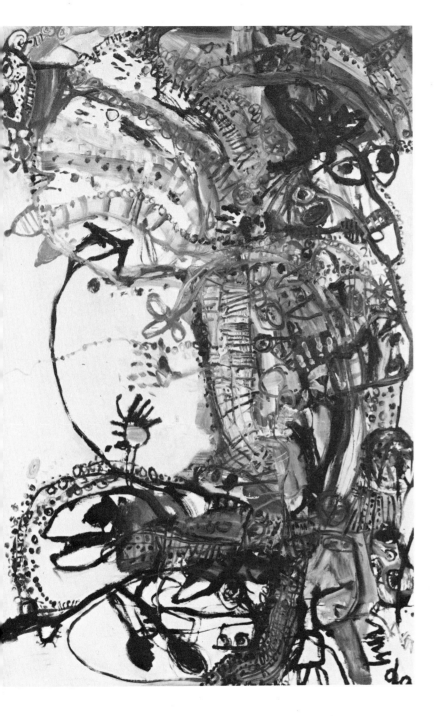

This same urgency can be seen in John Olsen's painting *Journey into the You Beaut Country No. 2,* which is in the Queensland Art Gallery. This picture was painted in 1961, and is one of a series of landscapes of the 'You Beaut Country'. When Olsen returned to Australia after a long period away in Europe, the excitement he felt for the particular nature of Australian landscape resulted in these paintings. He tells the story that one of his first impressions on returning to Australia was hearing someone on the wharf say "you beaut"; then he knew he was home, and that home was different. As with the aboriginal painting, the line has its own vital life; as it moves across the surface, it forms multiple images. It is at one and the same time the dry rough bark of a tree swarming with life, the horney back of a lizard, or a dry creek bed.

John Olsen (Australian, *b.* 1928).
*Journey into You Beaut Country No. 2,* 1961. Oil, 183 x 122 cms.
Brisbane, Queensland Art Gallery.

Jeffrey Smart (Australian, b. 1921).
*Morning Practice Baia*, 1969. Oil on
canvas, 58.5 x 81.3 cms.
Private collection, Switzerland.

Jeffrey Smart uses sharply focussed reality with a total sensation of real space. The painting is disturbing: there is a feeling of menace in the incongruity, it is almost as if time suddenly stood still, freezing the acrobat in mid-action, and the shadows on the wall.

64

Fred Williams (Australian, *b.*
1927). *Chopped Trees*, 1966. Oil
on canvas, 134.7 x 152.5 cms.
Collection of the Reserve Bank
of Australia.

This landscape of Fred Williams must be familiar to us all; the felled trees lying on the dry gold-green grass, the sparse standing trees looking like exclamation marks against the dusty sky. Notice that we can appreciate this picture on several levels: not only for the authentic feeling of the Australian bush, but also for the use of colour, and for the way the space works. Fred Williams has exploited the tricks that Australian light can play on our perception of things. See how the leaves of the small saplings seem to float above the horizon without any support from the ground. In contrast to the fragile saplings, the burnt trunks of larger trees seem to be floating right before our eyes. The space of the picture is what we make it, which can also apply to the way we feel space when looking at a real landscape.

Charles Blackman (Australian, *b.* 1928). *Sleep-Walking Nude,* 1968. Oil on canvas, 213.5 x 152 cms. Collection of Barbara Blackman.

In this painting, Charles Blackman uses an ambiguous space. Flat surfaces suddenly shoot back into space, then return to sit flat on the surface again, objects seem to float before your vision, and the sleepwalker dreams her way across the coloured rug where the cat lies sleeping. Blackman's use of pictorial space is your entry into the dream world, just as Lewis Carrol used the mirror in *Alice Through The Looking-Glass.*

Peter Powditch is interested in the way the venetian blinds cut across the image of the figure, leaving fragments which the mind pieces together. Notice how the space works; the slats of the blind sit on the picture plane dividing the surface into sections, the image of the figure stands close behind with the black background dropping sharply away.

Peter Powditch (Australian, *b.* 1942). *Venetian*, 1969. Oil on hardboard, 122 x 91.5 cms. Collection of Mr & Mrs J. Kahlbetzer.

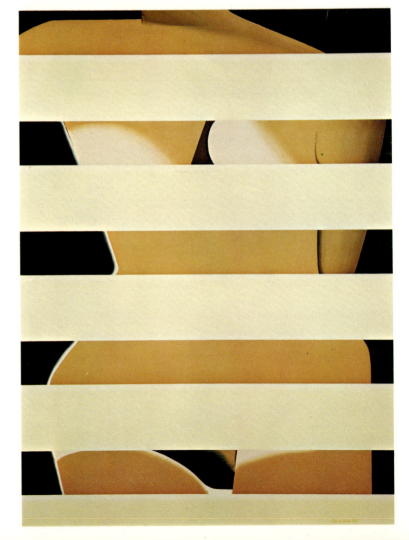

# chapter 4

# SPACE IN SCULPTURE

Unlike the painter, the sculptor is not dealing with an illusion of form on a flat surface, but with *an actual object in real space*. Because of this the material that the sculptor chooses can play an important part in the expressive nature of the work. We have seen how new building materials widened the scope of modern architects. In the same way today's sculptors are using new materials (such as aluminium, stainless steel, fibreglass, and plastics) to give shape to their ideas.

Some works of sculpture have a strong tactile (touch) quality. If you *look* at an object, for instance an apple, your eye interprets the shape, mass, and weight, by recording certain information: how the light moves across the form, how the colour seems more intense on the area that is closest to your eye. Now, if you close your eyes and take the apple into your hands, through the sense of *touch* you can experience the weight and shape of the *whole* object, not merely the one aspect that faces your eye. Have you noticed how you often long to touch pieces of sculpture in art galleries, in spite of all the 'Do Not Touch' signs? And how, even in large works, you can often imagine how it would feel if it were small enough to hold in the palm of your hand? Imagine holding in your hand this work by the English sculptor Henry Moore. However, not all forms invite us to experience their shape by the sense of touch. A spiky cactus for instance, has no inviting tactile quality.

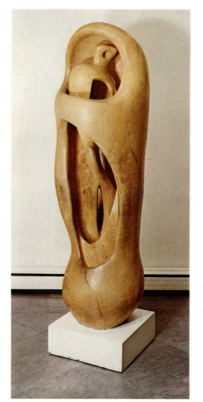

Henry Moore (English, b. 1898). *Internal & External Forms*, 1953–54. Albright-Knox Art Gallery, Buffalo, New York.

67

This bristly and aggressive character is the work of a Spanish sculptor, González. He manages to keep us at bay by his sharp and spiky tactile quality; so different from the smooth and sensuous tactile quality of the Henry Moore sculpture.

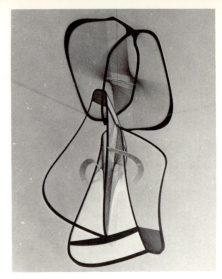

Auguste Rodin (French, 1840–1917). *Acrobats*, 1892–95. Bronze, 29 cms high, 8th of 12 castings. Brisbane, Queensland Art Gallery.

Naum Gabo (Russian, *b.* 1890, now living in U.S.A.). *Construction*. Aluminium, baked black plastic, gold wire, bronze mesh, steel wire. The Baltimore Museum of Art. Bequest of Saidie A. May.

Julio González (Spanish, 1876–1942). *Cactus Man 1*. Bronze, 64.5 cms high. Collection of Hans Hartung, Paris.

The supple, fluid forms of Rodin's *Acrobats* were modelled first in clay and later cast in bronze.

In this construction by the Russian, Gabo, one feels that the sculptor is modelling space, pushing space out, and holding it in, with the aluminium and plastic shapes. This work is suspended in the stairwell of the Baltimore Museum of Art. In the tall space that is the height of the whole building, one small area of space becomes complicated, tense, and alive.

2. The sculptor can *carve the form* out of a block of wood or stone. In this case the process is different, because in accordance with this method, the artist has to cut away the material from the outside, revealing the shape within.

The Italian Renaissance sculptor Michelangelo told us that he would look for some time at his block of marble until he could actually feel the form sitting inside. Then all he had to do was simply clear away the surrounding stone! A carving is limited by the size of the block of stone or wood, it cannot grow freely like a modelled form. It must also be in perfect balance because of the

Before dealing with how man has used space in sculpture, we will discuss some of the ways he can use his *materials:*

1. The sculptor can *model the form* he wishes to make out of some soft material such as clay or wax, building the shape out from the centre, and letting the form grow in a plastic (pliant, supple) way. If the artist wishes to transfer this model to some more permanent material, he can take a cast in bronze or some other metal from the wax or clay model.

physical weight of the stone. For instance, a standing figure in marble must have a support behind one leg, or the thin marble ankles would never support the weight of the marble torso above.

This is one of a series of four *Slaves* that Michelangelo carved in the early years of the sixteenth century (probably between 1530 and 1534). You can see the form of the man emerging from the great block of marble. He seems to be straining and struggling to break free from the weight of stone that holds him back. There is no doubt that these works are unfinished; they were first intended for a tomb for Pope Julius II, but were never used. However, they remained in Michelangelo's studio in this state for thirty years, and after his death in 1564, his nephew presented them to Cosimo I (a prince of the Medici family of Florence) who placed them in a garden grotto. This suggests that Michelangelo may have been satisfied with them in their unfinished state. These slaves were intended as images of the imprisoned soul, frustrated and hampered by the material body. Do you feel that the work illustrated here communicates this idea forcefully? Or do you think that the impact would be greater in a more finished state?

It is interesting to note that many of Michelangelo's late works are unfinished. As an older man his inner vision of the life and energy he wished to generate in his work, seems to prevent him from ever saying "That is now perfect and finished." It is almost as if for Michelangelo there was no end.

Michelangelo Buonarroti (Italian, 1475–1564). *The Awakening Slave*, probably 1530–34. Marble. Florence, Accademia.

69

Pablo Picasso (Spanish, 1881–1973). *Bulls Head*, 1943. Paris, Galerie Louise Leiris.

Picasso's inventive eye transforms a bicycle seat and handle bars into a bull's head.

A Brisbane schoolgirl (Davida Allan, age 17) made the clown balancing on a wheel chair after a visit to a local dump.

## Space in Sculpture from Ancient Egyptian Times to the Twentieth Century

The works of Egyptian sculpture that have survived for us to see are either large monumental works which are related to architecture (huge statues of seated pharaohs that stand at each

3. Another method used by modern sculptors is to *assemble* materials that already exist (scrap metal or 'found objects' such as springs, saucepan lids, bolts, screws, etc.). This method is related to modelling in that the form is built out by the process of adding one part to the next.

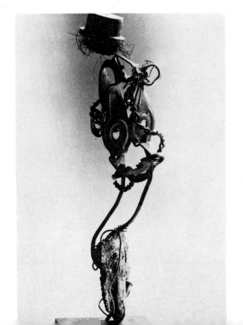

Davida Allan (Australian, b. 1953). *Clown on Wheel*, 1970. Made from parts of a rotary egg beater, wire, cogs, and other found junk.

*Young Girl Carrying a Ritual Offering*. Egyptian, 2000 B.C. Paris, The Louvre.

side of the temple doorway), or smaller tomb sculptures such as this statuette of a young girl carrying ritual offerings. The sculptor has made this young girl so that she can serve the dead king forever in his after-life. She steps forward into space to suggest the graceful walk of the girl, and the movement continues up into the raised arm which supports the basket on her head.

The Greeks also used sculpture not only as a means of giving extra life and meaning to architecture, but to create free-standing figures to serve a religious purpose, or to portray the spirit and ambitions of man. Two popular types of sculpture were figures of the *Kouros* (young man) and the *Kore* (young girl). These, like the Egyptian statutette of the young girl, represent people making offerings to the gods. The Kores show girls of Athens in the dress they wore for the festival of Panathenea, which took place every four years. At this time young girls of good family took part in a procession to the Parthenon, carrying in their hands sacrificial offerings to the goddess Athena. The statues were made to commemorate this offering, so that, in a sense, the goddess Athena could be forever served by her people.

This Kouros was made about 500 B.C., the offerings he once held in his hands have vanished. Like the Egyptian statue, he takes one step forward into space, in fact the whole stance of the figure is reminiscent of earlier Egyptian sculpture (it is thought that the Greeks were influenced by the Egyptians in these free-standing figures).

*Apollo.* Greek, *c.* 500 B.C.
Kouros in bronze, found in the
sea near Piombino, Italy. Paris,
The Louvre.

*Lapith and Centaur* (a battle of mythical creatures). Classical Greek, *c.* 435 B.C. Metope from the Parthenon. Marble, high relief, 142.3 cms square. Sculpture designed and supervized by Phidias. London, The British Museum.

Detail of *The Horsemen in the Panathenic Procession*. Classical Greek, *c.* 437 B.C. Frieze from the Parthenon. Marble, low relief, 99.2 cms high. Sculpture designed and supervized by Phidias. London, The British Museum.

Now let us see how the Greeks used sculpture to add vitality and meaning to their architecture.

Both these examples are from the exterior of the Parthenon. The one on the left is part of a long metope frieze which runs around the building above the outside columns. The one on the right is a section of a continuous frieze which ran around the outside wall of the cella (the enclosed part which held the statue of Athena). Remember that as you climb the steps of the Acropolis you see the Parthenon standing like a piece of sculpture on a pedestal of three steps. Your first view of the temple would be of the Doric columns and the metope frieze directly above. The sculptor has carved the figures well out from the background of stone *(high relief)* so that the play of light and the strongly cast shadows will

clearly outline the figures from a distance. These marble slabs are 1.2 metres high, and all represent some battle scene, symbolizing man's battle against the animal forces of nature in order to reach that elevated condition of mind and body which closely resembles the perfection of the gods. As we walk up the steps of the temple, past the row of outside columns, and look towards the cella, we see the second frieze. This time we see it, not from a distance, but from the covered walk which surrounds the cella. Since there is no need for a strong emphasis of light and shade, the sculptor has carved the shapes of horses and riders only a slight way out from the background of stone *(low relief)*. The legs of the horses and riders create a complicated forward energy which gives life and movement to the static wall of the cella.

These sculptures of classical Greek times set such a standard of perfection that the aim of later Roman sculptors was often merely to equal them.

When the Italian Renaissance sculptors looked back to the ancient works of Greece and Rome for inspiration, it was to these sculptures that they went. They marvelled at the way the ancient Greeks transformed marble and bronze into living form, which expressed so beautifully the Greeks' philosophy of the nobility of mind and body.

You will remember that, after the fall of the Roman Empire, the early Christian church became the unifying strength of Europe. The church banned the use of free-standing sculpture, because of its possible connection with paganism. (You will recall that Byzantine symbolism in painting was developed for the same reason.) During Romanesque and Gothic times in Europe, sculpture was used to add vitality to architecture, but seldom as an object existing in its own right.

On the left is a Romanesque doorway dating from about 1100 A.D., in which the sculptured form is a vital extension of the energy of the architectural form, but is still absolutely 'married' to the architecture. On the right is a Gothic figure of Eve, in which we can see the first signs of sculpture being considered to have a powerful expressive quality in its own right. Eve is very much at home in her architectural setting, but at the same time seems free to leave, and exist in her own right, should the spirit move her. Late Gothic sculptures perch in their niches, or on columns, like birds poised for flight. However, the actual separation from the building did not take place until the fifteenth century, in Renaissance times.

When Donatello modelled this figure of David in 1438 (four years after van Eyck painted his *Marriage of Jan Arnolfini and His Wife*) it was not only one of the first free-standing sculptures since classical times, but also one of the first nude figures to be represented since Roman times (Adam and Eve had been repre-

Pier with crossed lions and a prophet from the Church of St Peter, Moissac, France. *c.* 1100 A.D.

Figure of Eve on the exterior of the north end of the transept of Rheims Cathedral, France. Thirteenth century.

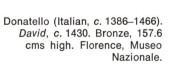

Donatello (Italian, *c.* 1386–1466). *David, c.* 1430. Bronze, 157.6 cms high. Florence, Museo Nazionale.

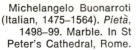

Michelangelo Buonarroti (Italian, 1475–1564). *Pietà*, 1498–99. Marble. In St Peter's Cathedral, Rome.

The Trevi Fountain, Rome. Eighteenth century. Neptune in a chariot drawn by two tritons. It is the custom to throw two coins into the fountain over one's shoulder, standing with one's back to it. The first coin brings a happy return to Rome, the second the fulfilment of a wish.

Gian Lorenzo Bernini (Italian, 1598–1680). *Apollo and Daphne,* 1622–24. Marble.

sented in the nude, but as a rule, modestly hiding their nudity). Although this figure is free-standing and does not belong to any architectural setting, it still has one important aspect—the front view. *David* could easily stand in a recess of a building and lose nothing of his grace and supple youthfulness.

However, apart from small sculptured objects such as salt cellars, candlesticks, incense burners, and chalices, this work marks the beginning of the independent sculptural work—work which asks for a total involvement with the object in its own environment, as opposed to the work which one stands back and looks at, as one would look at a painting.

This *Pietà,* which Michelangelo carved when he was twenty three, is also free-standing, but also has only one significant aspect —the front aspect that you see here. The back of the work holds no interest at all.

Bernini carved this life-size marble *Daphne and Apollo* more than a hundred years after Michelangelo carved his *Pietà.* In this work we can see further signs of sculpture's becoming independent from architecture. *Daphne and Apollo* does need to be seen from all sides. The movement of the figures pushes out into space, and space moves in and around the statue, becoming part of the life of the work. The ceiling of the Jesuit Church of Sant'Ignazio (page 46) belongs to the same period. Can you see a similar use of space and movement?

It was during the Baroque period that sculpture moved not only further away from an architectural setting, but moved out of churches and buildings altogether, into parks and city squares. Many of Europe's famous sculptured fountains and garden sculptures belong to this period (Rome's famous Trevi fountain, into which one traditionally throws a coin, is a late Baroque sculpture).

Auguste Rodin (French, 1840–1917). *The Burghers of Calais*, 1884–95. Bronze, about 214 cms high. Paris, Musée Rodin.

This group by the French sculptor Rodin shows six figures moving in space. Each one of the six figures is visible from any angle. In 1884 the town of Calais opened a competition for a monument commemorating the heroic burghers of Calais who sacrificed themselves for their city in the fourteenth century. Historical documents state that King Edward of England finally defeated the town, promising mercy to all except for six of the chief burghers, who were to come to him "bare headed, bare footed, with ropes about their necks, and the keys of the city and castle in their hands".

Rodin worked for ten years on this group and wanted the figures to stand on the soil without any pedestal, so that they might seem to be part of the population of the city square of Calais. Unfortunately this plan, not seeming practical to the municipal council, was not adopted. Rodin envisaged his figures moving in the space of the city square, as part of the actual life of the square. This statue was unveiled in Calais in 1895, four years before Cézanne painted his *Portrait of Ambroise Vollard*.

Alberto Giacometti (Swiss, 1901–1966). *City Square*, 1948. Bronze, 21.6 x 64.4 x 43.8 cms. Collection, The Museum of Modern Art, New York.

### Space in Twentieth Century Sculpture

This century has seen revolutionary ideas in sculpture as well as in painting and architecture. Today's sculptors, like all artists before them, are concerned with new attitudes and ideas that relate to the age in which they live. Whereas the Greek artist in his sculpture celebrated the human body as a symbol of the harmony and beauty of his ideal universe, and the horse as the most dynamic earthly power, today's artist is faced with the vast ingenuity of man in controlling force and motion with the precision machine.

In 1910 a group of contemporary artists issued a manifesto extolling the beauty and dynamics of modern technology: ". . . a roaring motor car . . . is more beautiful than the Victory of Samothrace."

We have already noted, on page 25, that modern technology has altered our concept of space, creating for us a new imaginative dimension. Many sculptural works of this century are concerned with space as a positive element of the work—as positive an element as mass.

Unlike Rodin, Giacometti in his *City Square* is not so much concerned with the figures themselves as with how each figure, intent on its own purpose and direction, marks out its own space. Although Rodin wanted his figures to move in the square of Calais, they are still conceived as a *mass,* Giacometti's *City Square* is a *space* for figures to move in. As you walk around this group, the shifting position of the figures creates a feeling of movement. In a strange silent way, they each move on a predestined course like satellites in space, never meeting, never making contact. In a very poetic way, Giacometti makes a comment on the feeling of isolation one often has when moving in a crowd of people, but the work requires 'audience participation'—just standing back and looking is not enough. If you compare this piece of sculpture with Giacometti's painting on page 55, or with Rembrandt's painting of St Anastasius on page 47, you will notice a similar interest in the relation between man and the space that surrounds him.

Boccioni made this *Development of a Bottle In Space* in 1912, about the same time as Picasso was working on his cubist pictures. Like Giacometti, he is also interested in space. But instead of making you aware of this by his positioning objects in space, he is more interested in how space 'moves around' an object, and in how the eye sees space and understands it. Look at any object in the room, feeling out the space with your eyes. Then think how you could transfer this sensation to a solid object. Boccioni is giving form to the direction that his eye has taken as it moved across the table, around the shape of the bottle and into the volume of the bottle, through the transparent glass. His eye then swept around the outside space, which then becomes the curve of bronze which seems to hold the bottle in position. This sculpture represents, not so much an object sitting on a table, as how our eye sees that object in space.

You will remember that painters were also becoming more interested in the way we see things, and how our memory stores information, than in the factual record of the object itself.

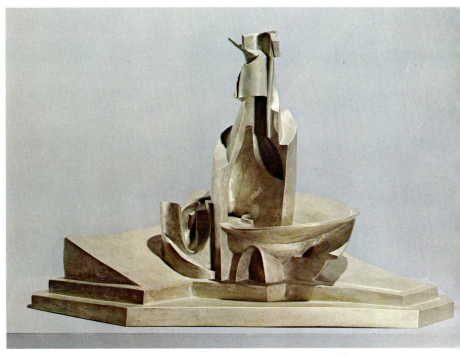

Umberto Boccioni (Italian, 1882–1916). *Development of a Bottle in Space,* 1912, Silvered Bronze, 38.1 x 32.7 x 60.3 cms. Collection, The Museum of Modern Art, New York, Aristide Maillol Fund.

Diagram showing the manner in which the eye explores the object and the space it occupies: the sensation and movement of vision.

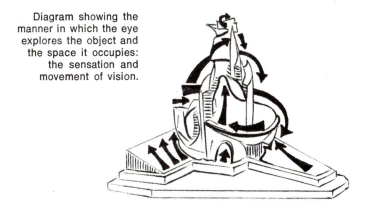

Constantin Brancusi (Rumanian, 1876–1957). *Bird in Space*, 1928(?). Polished bronze, unique cast, 137.3 cms high. Collection, The Museum of Modern Art, New York.

When Brancusi came to Paris from Rumania in 1904, his work attracted the attention of Rodin, who asked him to become his assistant. Brancusi refused, saying that nothing will grow in the shade of a great tree. He realized that he had to develop his own ideas inlependently. This polished bronze of *Bird in Space* (1928) is one of several works on the same subject. He is not concerned with giving shape to the bird itself, but to the sensation we get when we think of a bird soaring through space. The material that he has

chosen—the highly polished bronze—accentuates the feeling of a form slipping through space. It has the smooth efficiency of a piece of precision machinery and seems to predict man's flight through cosmic space which was to come later.

When the American sculptor Alexander Calder designed this work for the courtyard of the Moderna Museet (Modern Museum) in Stockholm, he did not suggest movement in space, but made use of actual movement, in this case controlled by a motor. This is a piece of environmental sculpture, in that the moving shapes of colour have been designed to add life and energy to the whole environment of the open square. The clear, flat sheets of colour (blue, yellow, orange, red, and black) keep interchanging, and re-arranging their order as the motor rotates the movable parts at different speeds. Our fascination with the moving and changing parts is the same fascination we feel from the movement of water in a fountain.

Alexander Calder (American, b. 1898). *Four Elements*, 1961. Monumental mobile. Moderna Museet, Stockholm.

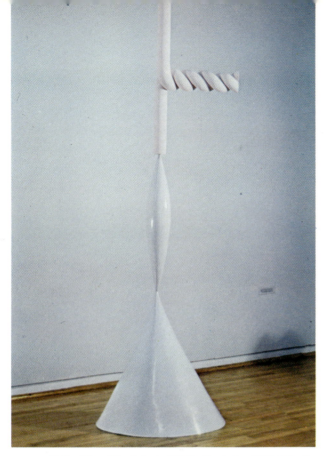

Philip King (English, *b*. 1934). *Tra-la-la*, 1963. Plastic, 274.3 x 76.2 cms. The Tate Gallery, London.

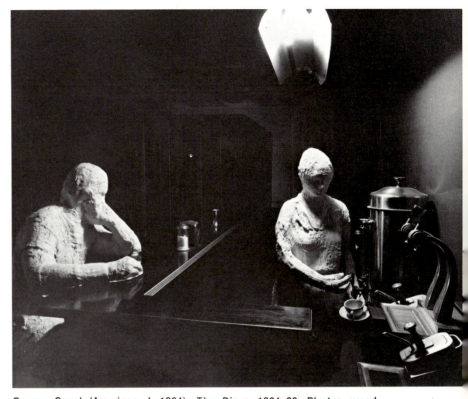

George Segal (American, *b*. 1924). *The Diner*, 1964–66. Plaster, wood, chrome, formica, masonite, life-size figures. Collection, The Walker Art Centre, Minneapolis.

The British sculptor Phillip King makes use of new materials (plastic and fibreglass) and colour. His shapes seem to float in the environment of the room, without weight or gravity.

The fine vertical shapes of this work balance precariously on the cone base, the horizontal twist creating a strange in-balance, which adds to the breathless poise of the column—rather like a ballet dancer who pauses for a moment in mid-movement, and for a second seems to defy gravity.

King is making full use of plastics. He could never make these things in stone, wood, or metal.

Whereas Phillip King takes pleasure in making his plastics hover in space, twisting or pouring themselves across the space of a room, the American pop sculptor George Segal is interested in a new reality. Everything in Segal's construction is real—the diner stools, the coffee urn, even the plaster figures are plaster casts taken from real people. The only thing that is not real is the fact that nothing changes, nothing moves—time stands still. The Bernini statue of *Daphne and Apollo* suggests the moment before and the moment after, but in this tableau by Segal there seems to be no before and no after. We see this same quality in the paintings of

79

Segal. *Execution*, mid-1960s. Plaster, life-size figures. The Vancouver Art Gallery.

the Australian painter Jeffrey Smart (page 64). The closer Segal gets to actual reality, the more unreal the situation becomes. Michelangelo's *Pietà* is, in a sense, equally real. However, not only does the subject matter set it apart, it is conceived and presented as a work of art, and we look at it as such. The 'spooky' thing about Segal's sculpture is that he makes few concessions to the 'work of art', and makes no separation between the object and the audience. There is no frame or pedestal. The work just 'happens' in the space of the room, like any ordinary event.

Although Segal makes few concessions to our preconceived idea of what a work of art should be, he is still doing what all artists in the past have done: that is, *selecting* from his world and then *presenting* what his eye and mind select in such a positive way that it can increase our awareness and sensibilities.

In this work, Segal's comment is upon human suffering, injustice, and death. He forces us into a personal encounter with brutality. By taking plaster casts from real people, he is closing in the gap between the audience and the work of art. He does not want us to be diverted or distracted by technical skills; he wants us to see what it is—not how it has been done. The four figures occupy a tangible space, continuous with the space of the audience, and of the same size as the audience—too close and too real for escape.

## Space in Australian Sculpture

It is only in fairly recent years that sculpture has played a prominent role in the Australian art scene. Robert Hughes (art critic and historian) once said "Sculpture has always been the poor cousin at the feast of Australian painting". However, this situation is rapidly changing, and one factor that has helped to bring about this change is the emergence of a group of sculptors whose work has sufficient authority, assurance, and vitality to place sculpture in Australia on a firm and established footing. One sculptor who has played a very prominent role in this sense is Robert Klippel. In his early work, Klippel was absorbed in the relationship between organic and mechanical shapes, working mainly in metal or wood. However, by 1960 he was creating 'junk art' from pieces of adding-machines, typewriter bars, pinions, gears, wheels, and pistons. By being welded together, these pieces lose the implications of their original use and are transformed into a new life.

In this work, called simply *Sculpture,* there is still evidence of Klippel's early interest in the relation between living forms and machine forms. The structure seems to grow up from its base and from its skeleton centre send feelers out into space like a sea anemone. Klippel would not be able to make a similar form from any other material, it needs the complicated ready-made shapes of the scrap heap.

80

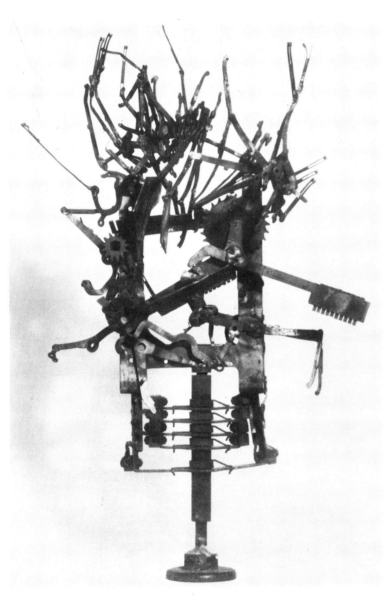

Clive Murray-White uses aluminium for these three slightly dome shaped discs. They are placed low on the ground because the sculptor has used the floor in the same way as a painter uses the picture plane—that is, he makes the discs react in a spatial way to the horizontal plane of the ground.

Do you notice that you can look at this work and experience two different spaces working at the same time? The three discs move away from your eye, marking out a horizontal space on the ground plane, the diminishing size of the discs exaggerating the normal effect of perspective. At the same time, they can seem to float vertically one above the other, marking out a vertical space directly above the larger disc.

Murray-White has made the smallest section flat so that it traps the light on its surface in a uniform way, making it lighter in tone than the others—the lighter tone then seems to float towards the eye. From the other side, it works in exactly the same way. How-

Clive Murray White (Australian). Untitled Sculpture. Aluminium, 127 x 99 x 53 cms.

Robert Klippel (Australian, *b.* 1920). Metal Sculpture, 1963. 'Junk', 41.9 cms high. Collection of Robert Hughes.

ever, the perspective is then reversed, and it is the size of the larger shape which makes it seem to come forward and float above the small disc. Painters as well as sculptors can be interested in a similar ambiguity of our perception of shape and space—producing this sensation with line, tone, and colour, as in this painting by the English artist, David Hockney.

Clement Meadmore is an Australian; he has been working in New York since 1963. In both these works the large steel shapes twist and turn in space. With apparent weightlessness they seem to effortlessly mark out a fluid movement in contrast to the rigid city environment for which they were designed. By using steel they suit the mood of the modern city, yet their organic life suggests a freedom of spirit which we do not usually associate with steel. Meadmore prepares a model from polystyrene, and, from this and working drawings, steel fabricators produce a *maquette* (small model). The full-scale steel sculpture is based on this maquette. *Awakening* was designed for the A.M.P. Building in Melbourne, and creates a forceful impact of twisting shape and subtle changes of light and shade.

David Hockney (English, *b.* 1937). *Marriage of Styles No. 2*, 1963. Oil on canvas, 198 x 228.2 cms. National Gallery of Victoria, presented by the Contemporary Art Society of London, 1965.

Meadmore. *Curl.* Steel.

Clement Meadmore (Australian, *b.* 1929). *Awakening*, 1968. Steel. In the courtyard of the A.M.P. Building, Melbourne.

# SECTION TWO

# STRUCTURE AND FORM

In the previous section we saw how man has used space in order to express an idea, or to serve a particular need. In this section we will discuss the *structure* and *form* man has used in order to make space possible. It would serve no purpose for the Gothic architect to dream of the inspiring interior space of the Gothic cathedral unless he could build a structure to enclose that space.

Before looking at this aspect of building, painting, and sculpture, we should first try to understand exactly what we mean by structure and form.

*Structure* is the building up of parts to make a whole. If you were given six blocks, you could make a structure by piling them one on top of the other, or by lying them end to end on the table, or by building a pyramid of them. From the same six identical parts you could make many different structures, simply by arranging them in different ways. You yourself are an amazingly complex structure, and part of an equally complex structure—each cell of your body builds up each part, each part builds up the whole: the person you see in the mirror every morning. You, in turn, are part of the structure of your family and home, which is part of the structure of the suburb and city, and so it goes on. When John Donne in the seventeenth century said "No man is an island entire unto itself" he was making reference to the structure of society.

*Form* is simply the shape of a thing. For instance, we could talk of the form or shape of an apple. We could line up five apples in a row and notice that each possesses a similar spherical form; they belong to the same family of shape. However, we would not find two apples exactly the same, some are bigger than others, some are rounder than others. While belonging to the same family of shape, each apple has an individual form. In the same way each Gothic cathedral in Europe is different and individual, while adhering to the same basic form.

A musical composition should also have form, it should be arranged in such a way that we can comprehend its 'shape', even though it is not a visible object like an apple or a vase. By this I do not mean that it is necessary to have a rigid shape or form to things. For instance, when you dance, the form is provided by the rhythm and time of the music, but within that general form all sorts of individual improvisations are possible. We will think of form as the shape of a thing, and of structure as the arrangement of the parts that make that shape. To use the example of the apple again, its form is the shape we see, its structure the molecules and atoms that make the core, flesh, and skin.

We will start by looking at the structure and form of things in our everyday environment.

# chapter 5

# THE STRUCTURE AND FORM OF OUR ENVIRONMENT

The appearance of natural forms is fashioned by *necessity*—the shape of a fish is in the evolutionary process of becoming the perfect shape to move smoothly through water; its colour is either a camouflage against the predatory attack of other fish, or to attract attention for mating—a signalling device. The great buttress trees of the rain forest are another example. Their supporting root structure allows the tree to climb to enormous heights to reach the light. This same process of adaption of shape to suit external circumstances can be seen in inanimate objects. The river pebble is shaped by the friction of water and river gravel. Like all things in nature, it is in the process of becoming—nothing is static or 'finished'.

Many aspects of man-made things are similar to shapes in nature—they are the outcome of a practical necessity. The beautiful lines of a jet aeroplane are not there to please the eye, but to allow the aeroplane to function properly. If the streamlined shapes of the aeroplane, racing car, or speed boat (in which the form closely follows the function) should be applied to other objects of different function, then the result is a *fashionable style*. For instance, a family sedan car with upswept tail fins—as these cars seldom need to travel at more than 110 kilometres per hour there is no real need for such elaborate streamlining. You must have seen examples of this kind of fashionable styling at some time—for example, the streamlined shape of a kitchen utensil, an object which rarely needs to fly through the air with a minimum of wind resistance.

A design which is perfectly right and fitting for one situation, could well be altogether wrong in another. The smooth efficiency of office furniture and fittings can be chilling if used in a home, where we expect to see some evidence of the character and life of a family. We have seen this same stylistic adaption happen to jeans, which originated as tough and comfortable work trousers, were adopted by city dwellers for the same reason, and then exploited by manufacturers, thus gradually losing their original rough but tough functional qualities and becoming a fashionable style with a built-in tattered and faded look.

If you make a study of the development of motor car design from the very first models to recent designs, it is interesting to see just how many changes have actually increased the efficiency of the car (I am referring to the shape of the car, not to its engine), and how many changes are stylistic, catering for fashionable taste but serving no real purpose. Take into account details such as dashboard designs, tail lights, fenders, etc., remembering the functional aspect of these things; for instance, the purpose of the dashboard dials is for quick and foolproof reading. When you

Modern car design — a car in a salesroom.

Milton Moon (Australian, *b.* 1926) Teapot, 1968. Handthrown pottery.

A factory-made enamel teapot (or kettle). Pleasant to look at and to use, but lacking in individuality.

The tea-pot on the left was made by the Australian potter Milton Moon; the one on the right is factory-made. Both are functional, but Milton Moon's hands have created a unique object with that elusive quality of individual life and vitality which the machine cannot give.

have completed the survey, select the make which has catered most efficiently for all the functional aspects of a motor car, and see if it is also the most pleasing shape visually.

Unfortunately, mass production of basic designs, while satisfying the practical needs of man, makes no room for his imaginative needs—to express an individuality through personal objects. If the Australian railways need a cheap unbreakable tea cup that can be stacked away in the smallest amount of space, then the obvious solution is a totally functional shape which caters for all these needs. However, as cheaper, more efficient, mass produced items appear, so the popularity of the individual hand-made article grows. A hand-thrown bowl or jug, a hand-worked leather bag, even silk-screened T-shirts, can become a means of expressing an individual taste in a world of mass production. When you decorate your jeans with coloured stitching, or your car with stickers, you are making an individual mark on a mass produced item.

The T & G Building in Adelaide — a purely functional edifice.

86

The human instinct for the personal touch can also be seen in architecture. Compare the two buildings illustrated here. The building on the left fulfils all the functional requirements of an insurance building. Gaudi's Sagrada Familia (Church of the Holy Family) in Barcelona, although unfinished, is a monument to that element of human fantasy and imagination which is particularly important in a world that is generally shaped by the machine.

Antonio Gaudi (Spanish, 1852–1926). Sagrada Familia (The church of the Holy Family). 1882–      . Barcelona. Plans were originally Gothic revival, but the building becomes more and more Gaudi's personal style from storey to storey. Here is the frantic desire for the unprecedented, the faith in the creative individual, the delight in the arbitrary curve, and the keen interest in the possibilities of materials.

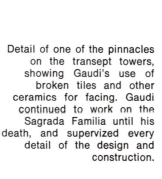

Detail of one of the pinnacles on the transept towers, showing Gaudi's use of broken tiles and other ceramics for facing. Gaudi continued to work on the Sagrada Familia until his death, and supervized every detail of the design and construction.

The four great towers terminate in sculptured features of fantastic shape, covered in coloured mosaics. The three pointed gables over the main doorways drip imitation snow, carved out of stone. In fact, the whole structure is a complex and lively fantasia of colour and form. In areas where the architect uses mosaics of glass and ceramic, he often insets fragments of broken plates, fragments of china dolls and bottles, anything to give extra life or colour to a particular area.

If at this point you feel like asking "But what *is* good design?" I think the answer could be: "Any form or structure that has been shaped to a *real* need; either a functional need or an imaginative one." Let us see how this definition can be applied to a personal environment, a small town, and a city.

87

The Australian artist Ian Fairweather (*b*. Scotland, 1890) at work in the studio he built himself on Bribie Island.

A more usual personal environment — the interior of a home in Pullenvale, Brisbane.

**A personal environment.** If our immediate environment works in a practical way for us as individuals, its form being dictated by our real needs (and here we must try to be honest and not be too influenced by what fashionable media tell us we *should* need), then the result will be pleasing because of its sense of 'rightness' for that particular situation.

In order to think and work as he feels he must, Australian artist Ian Fairweather has built his own environment on Bribie Island in Moreton Bay. Fairweather needs to work in seclusion,

freeing himself from the limiting and time-consuming luxuries of life, which most of us feel to be essential and central to living; by refusing to become the owner of material possessions, he ensures that objects never possess him. The simple dignity of his situation has a sense of rightness.

Although in complete contrast, the environment shown on the right also has been shaped to serve the needs of another, though totally different, human being, and is therefore also visually pleasing.

This suburban area has been allowed to develop slowly and naturally, and so has an individuality lacking in many large-scale developments where an arbitrary plan is imposed without thought on a flattened and cleared landscape.

Winter Park, a cluster housing development at Doncaster, Melbourne, designed to take account of the existing land contour, and the large old gum trees. There are twenty houses in the development, on strata titles.

**A small town.** You will recall that Le Corbusier was moved by the sight of small Mediterranean fishing villages, built to suit the individual needs of each family and adapted to the existing contour of the land. These villages have evolved naturally to suit existing local conditions, just as the shape of the fish has evolved. However, had a land developer first moved in with his bulldozer and a 'spec' builder built a village of houses designed for the 'average' man on the conveniently flattened landscape, then there is every possibility that another boring wasteland would have resulted.

Although these suburbs may look silly on a Greek island, they are right in their *own situation*. Their form has also been decided by the nature and contour of the land, and by the needs of the people who live there.

89

This shop verandah in Helidon, Queensland, provides a cool respite from the glare of the sun.

The 'modern' design of the Laidley Commonwealth Bank provides no protection from the heat of the sun or from downpours of rain.

A street scene in the country town of Rosewood, Queensland.

In the same way, the structure of a town should be governed both by man's need for functional efficiency in a specific situation, and by his need for personal expression and identity. These particular needs will vary with the geographic situation, and with the nature of the town and of the people who live and work in it. This is one reason why it would be a great shame if Australian towns and cities were to become too influenced by overseas equivalents. A certain degree of this world-wide uniformity is inevitable. But if town planners are sensitive to the unique needs of each situation, then the structure should function in a personal way and have that pleasing sense of rightness which is good design.

The first two photographs are of small country towns, where awnings protect the pavement from the hot sun—so comfortable and convenient for the people living in this particular climate and situation. The new 'modern' look of the building in the third photograph may satisfy a need for status and 'progress', but on the human level it has ceased to function as effectively.

**A city.** On a different scale, the same thing can happen to the larger cities. In the mad scramble to keep pace with 'progress', we stand a chance of losing all sense of personal identity. It is interesting to take a look at your own city or town to see how many structures and areas are the result of that unique situation—the people, the climate, the locality, the economy—in short, the way of life.

# chapter 6

# STRUCTURE AND FORM
# IN ARCHITECTURE

When early man first left the shelter of the caves, he built for himself a shelter—a man-made 'cave'. However, the first *monument* he built was a tomb to shelter the dead. These neolithic tombs are called *dolmens* and consist of huge rough-hewn uprights of stone with a horizontal slab resting on top. For the first time man makes a structure large enough and strong enough to withstand the effects of time and so outlive his own temporary nature. He has built himself a monument with the same method of building that a child uses when playing with blocks—by laying a beam across two upright supports.

This early Egyptian tomb is known as a *mastaba*. You can see that the neolithic dolmen has become more refined, but the basic construction is the same. Now the body is placed in a subterranean chamber and the structure becomes a protective block, which also marks the place of burial.

A neolithic (*c.* 3500 B.C.–*c.* 1600 B.C.) dolmen — a primitive demonstration of man's desire for the monumental and imposing.

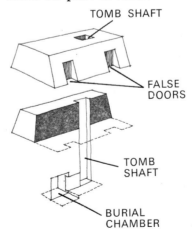

TOMB SHAFT

FALSE DOORS

TOMB SHAFT

BURIAL CHAMBER

A mastaba — an early Egyptian sunken sealed tomb.

When King Zoser, the great and powerful pharoah of the Old Kingdom, made himself a spectacular monument by placing six of these mastabas one on top of the other in diminishing size, he built the first step pyramid—the forerunner of the great pyramid of Cheops.

The step pyramid of Zoser (c. 2778 B.C.) was built of limestone. It is 126 x 105 square metres in area and 61 metres high. The earliest known large-scale stone monument.

You will remember that when the Egyptians built a monument to house their gods they erected a secret and enclosed shrine. In front of this they built a vast dimly-lit hall to symbolize the majesty and mystery of the secret place beyond. The method they used to

A reconstruction of the hypostyle hall at the great Temple of Ammon at Karnak. The tall central columns are just over 21 metres high and 3.6 metres in diameter, and the side columns are 12.8 metres in height and 2.8 metres diameter. A model in The Metropolitan Museum of Art, New York, Levi Hale Willard Bequest, 1890.

build this hall was the same simple construction of flat roofing beams of stone supported by stone columns. This method is known as *post and lintel construction* or, in architectural terms, *trabeated style* (trabs = a beam). This is a most efficient means of building, but it involves one important restriction. Until the technology of this century invented the reinforced concrete beam and the steel girder, this method of roofing a large area required numerous supports (rather like the stumps which support raised Queensland homes). If the architects of the past used wood for their roof beams, they were restricted by the length of sturdy trees; if they used stone, they were restricted by the amount of stress an unsupported length of stone can take.

If we see the ruins of these great temple halls today, with strong light streaming in through broken walls and roof, it is difficult to reconstruct the original atmosphere, which relied a great deal on the gloom of restricted lighting. There was no strong side-light from windows in the walls. Instead, the architects raised the level of the roof in the centre of the hall and fitted stone blocks with vertical slits into the space between the two roof levels. The light filtered down through these slits into the hall below. This method of letting light in between two roof levels is known as *clerestory* lighting.

As you can imagine, a hall which consists of a forest of vast columns supporting the roof is not the ideal place for a large

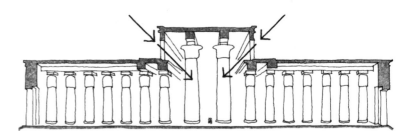

A diagram showing how clerestorey lighting works.

number of people to witness a ceremony. The architects solved the problem by building one or two large open courtyards in front of the hall. These courtyards were used on rare occasions when the ritual involved large numbers of people, such as the coronation of a pharoah, or the annual festival of a god. The reliable climate of Egypt made it possible to enclose large areas without having to face the problem of a roof.

The Greeks did not shroud their gods in mystery and darkness, but conceived of them as more approachable 'super-beings'—they therefore built different structures to suit these different ideas.

When the ancestors of the ancient Greeks built a shrine for their god or goddess, they built a simple rectangular room of sun-dried clay bricks. To protect the walls from the weather they built a wooden roof which projected well beyond the walls on all sides, and was supported on wooden posts.

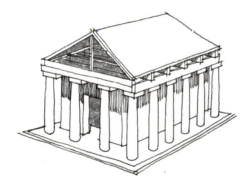

An archaic Greek shrine, built of mud and wood. The archaic, or ancient period was from *c.* 700 B.C. until *c.* 480 B.C. when it developed into the Classical period.

By the time the Greeks had become a great and powerful nation, they were no longer building with mud and wood, but with strong and permanent white marble. However, the form of the traditional temples had, by this time, become a style, and Greek architects

continued to build the protective shelter around the marble cella, even though it no longer needed protection from the weather. This is an interesting case of a form, which had its origins in necessity, becoming a refined style.

You can see that the wooden posts have become marble columns with carved vertical grooves *(flutings)*—a stylized abstraction of the vertical grain of wood. At the point where the upward thrust of the column meets the downward thrust of the weight from above the architects have placed a marble 'cushion', known as a *capital*. If you press your finger into the palm of your hand, then place a rubber or some flat 'cushion' between your finger and hand, you will be able to feel how the pressure is dispersed over a larger area. Directly above these capitals is a marble beam made up of sections of marble, each being supported by a column. This marble beam replaces the wooden beam of the archaic temple which was laid across the top of the upright posts to hold the cross timbers of the roof. The marble slabs above this beam with the projecting vertical bands are known as *triglyphs* and are a decorative feature based on the cut ends of the wooden cross beams of the old temple.

The Parthenon as it is today, looking up to the entablature. Classical Greek period, Doric style, built *c.* 447–432 B.C. The columns are 10.4 metres high and 1.9 metres in diameter at the base.

Even the small marble projections below the triglyphs are a stylized version of the pegs which once held the old structure together. The carved *metope* slabs (see page 72) were fixed into place between the triglyphs.

Diagram of triglyphs and metopes from the entablature.

The cella of the Parthenon was 19.2 metres wide—too wide to be spanned by a single unsupported wooden beam. The architects solved this problem by placing a double row of columns inside the space of the cella. The diameter at the base of the outside columns is 1.9 metres. If these columns were moved inside, they would have taken up too much of the interior space. Hence, rather than spoil the proportions of the column by making it long and narrow, the architects placed two smaller columns one on top of the other.

NAOS

AMBULATORY

A transverse section through the Parthenon, showing the row of double columns in the cella.

Just as the basic, functional form of the archaic temple became elaborate and refined, so the shape of the column was changed and decorated by later architects. Notice that the Ionic and Corinthian columns have become taller and more slender, making it necessary to have a cushion of stone at each end—as well as a capital, they each have a moulded base.

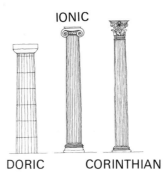

IONIC

DORIC          CORINTHIAN          The three classical Greek orders.

It is interesting to see that these columns have been used again and again by later generations. The Romans borrowed them from the Greeks, the Renaissance architects revived their use in Europe, and we see them used again on the facades of many municipal buildings of the nineteenth and early twentieth century.

It was the Romans who first solved the problem of roofing a large area without obstructing the interior space with supports. They achieved this with the *vault* and the *dome*.

Suppose you were to place a flat plank of wood across two bricks and then stand in the middle of the plank, all your weight would be directed down at that point where you stand, and it is

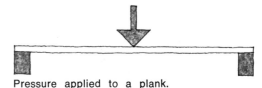

Pressure applied to a plank.

there that the plank will break if it is too weak to support your weight. However, if you were to place a curved piece of wood across two supports and stand on that, then your weight would be directed down the curve of wood to the two supports, and it is the supports that will topple over if they are not strong enough. You can see now the value of the vaulted ceiling. All the weight of the vault itself and any roof structure above will be directed down and out to the walls, and, as long as those walls are strong enough, there is no need for any support in the middle. This principle of an arch or curve dispersing weight down and out to side supports can be seen in many natural and man-made objects.

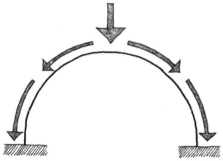

Pressure applied to a curved surface.

St John's Chapel in the White Tower of The Tower of London. 1090–1278 A.D. The rounded Romanesque arches are an example of a weight-carrying structure dispersing the load out and down onto side supports.

Look at this diagram of the skeleton of a horse. Note that the inverted arch of the spine is strengthened by thickened vertebra at the two points where the arch meets the upright supports of the front and back legs. There is added strengthening above the front legs to cope with the weight of the cantilevered head.

The skeleton of a horse: the areas of greatest stress have the strongest vertebrae.

Here the deck of a bridge is being supported by a concrete arch. Notice the similar strengthening of structure where the ends of the arch meet its support.

A bridge consists basically of two parts — the deck, which is a continuation of the road, and the supporting arch. The arch supporting this bridge is strengthened at its ends, as that is where the weight is carried.

95

The curve of the human skull is the perfect shape for dispersing the impact of any blow. If we had square heads not many of us would have survived the knocks and bumps of childhood.

A vault can be built with bricks, which are laid on a wooden framework until the last brick has been cemented into position; the bricks are then wedged firmly against each other and the wooden support can be removed. Or it can be made with cement, in which case the cement is poured into wooden shuttering built to the curve of the vault, and supported from below by scaffolding, all of which is removed when the cement has set hard.

The Greeks never used cement. The marble blocks of the Parthenon are secured together by wrought iron cramps and dowels, protected by molten lead.

The discovery that small fragments of stone or broken bricks, set in a mortar of lime and a special sand (*pozzolana*, a type of earth found in all the volcanic regions of Italy), would set into a rock hard composition, gave the Romans a wonderful new building material. Skilled craftsmen would see to the outer casing and the erection of the temporary wooden centerings for the arches and vaults, but the purely mechanical task of dumping alternate layers of mortar and broken stones, which would solidify into concrete, was performed by local slaves.

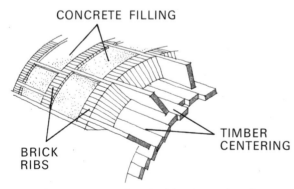

CONCRETE FILLING

BRICK RIBS

TIMBER CENTERING

The method of vault construction used by the ancient Romans —wooden shuttering, brick ribs, and cement filling.

When the Emperor Hadrian built the Pantheon (120–124 A.D.), his architects made use of this new building material. In order to support the enormous weight of concrete in the dome, which is more than 1.2 metres thick in its upper part, a massive foundation 4.5 metres deep supports a circular concrete wall. This wall, 6.1 metres thick, is two tiers high to the springing (the base) of the hemispherical dome, but a third tier on the outside provides rigid and weighty haunches to prevent the weight of the dome from splitting outwards. This is why Roman domes always appear saucer-shaped from the outside, though hemispherical inside. The weight of the dome is reduced by the circular opening which lets in light, and by five tiers of coffers (square recesses let into the thickness of the concrete). The structure is a brilliant piece of engineering, carefully devised to meet every kind of stress and strain.

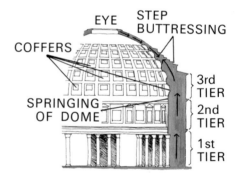

EYE  STEP BUTTRESSING

COFFERS

SPRINGING OF DOME

3rd TIER

2nd TIER

1st TIER

A transverse section through the Pantheon, showing how the weight of the dome is supported.

Inside, the walls are lined with marble and porphyry; and outside they were once faced with gleaming white pentelic marble. The dome exterior, and the lower portion which is formed in steps, were covered with gilded bronze plates until they were removed to Constantinople in 655 A.D.

It was Byzantine architects in the fifth century A.D. who made the next great step in the development of the dome. The Romans had solved the problem of roofing a large, unbroken area with a dome; but they could not support that dome on anything but circular walls of enormous strength and thickness. The Byzantine architects devized a means of supporting a dome on four massive piers, which meant that they could use the dome, but were no longer limited to circular buildings. This method of dome construction is called *pendentive construction*. The four piers which are to support the dome are linked by four arches. The base of the dome sits on the apex of these four arches, the weight of the dome being directed down the curve of the arch to the supporting pier.

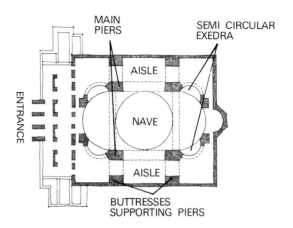

The ground plan of the Hagia Sophia.

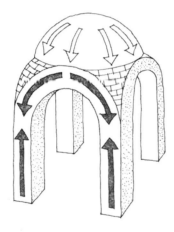

The principle of pendentive construction, where the dome rests on pendentives.

The space between the arches and the circular base of the dome is first filled with mortared bricks (these are wedged in between the curve of the arches, and cannot shift) which gives a continuous circular support for the base of the dome. These triangular spaces are known as *pendentives*.

The plan of Hagia Sophia consists of a central space 32.6 metres square with four massive piers supporting four semicircular arches upon which rests the main dome. To east and west of the central

dome, half domes are built into the supporting arches of the main dome, the space thus enclosed forming a great oval nave. To the north and south of the nave are two-storeyed aisles over 15 metres wide, the upper storey being the women's gallery. These side aisles bring the ground plan of the whole building to approximately a square.

A side-elevation of Hagia Sophia.

97

This is a plan of a Roman *basilica,* or law court. It is almost as if the outside columns of the Greek temple have moved inside, and the ambulatory or passage way that was around the outside of the Greek temple structure, is now part of the interior. I mention this building now because it is the ancestor of the early Christian church in the west. The form of the basilica was borrowed by the early Christians, partly because it had no connections with pagan religions, but mainly because the design is ideally suited to house a congregation. As you can see, the large central section is free of supports and can accommodate a large number of people, and the two side aisles allow free passage to any part of the building. The semicircular section at either end held seats for judge and jury.

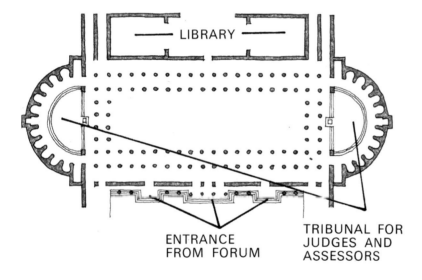

A typical ground plan of a Roman Basilica, or law court.

If you compare the plan of a typical early Christian church with the plan of the Roman basilica you can notice many similarities, but also some changes. The entrance is now at the end of the

98

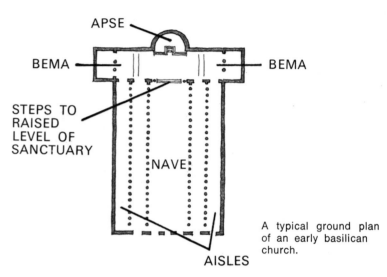

A typical ground plan of an early basilican church.

building and there is only one semicircular section or *apse.* Imagine walking into the Roman basilica from the forum. You are standing at once in the middle of the building. To left and right, the building is in perfect symmetrical balance. However, in an early Christian church, one would need to walk the length of the *nave* in order to reach the significant part of the building—the high altar framed by the half dome of the semicircular apse. To provide light and air to the central nave, which was enclosed on each side by the passageways or aisles, the architects used clerestory windows by raising the roof level of the nave above the two side aisles.

It was this plan that was enlarged, added to, made more noble and impressive by later generations, until it reached a peak of structural perfection and grandeur in Gothic architecture. In the diagram you can see the changes that took place to the structure of the Christian church.

The Gothic nave is not only much taller, but the walls have become thinner with enlarged clerestory windows designed for stained glass. The weight of the pointed vaults and wooden roof

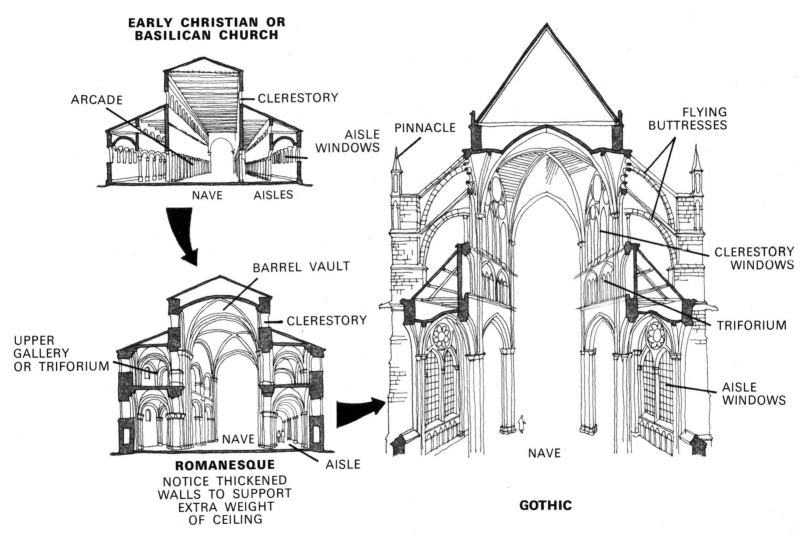

**EARLY CHRISTIAN OR BASILICAN CHURCH**

ARCADE

CLERESTORY

AISLE WINDOWS

NAVE    AISLES

BARREL VAULT

CLERESTORY

UPPER GALLERY OR TRIFORIUM

NAVE

**ROMANESQUE**
NOTICE THICKENED WALLS TO SUPPORT EXTRA WEIGHT OF CEILING

AISLE

PINNACLE

FLYING BUTTRESSES

CLERESTORY WINDOWS

TRIFORIUM

AISLE WINDOWS

NAVE

**GOTHIC**

The development of the Gothic Cathedral from the early Christian and Romanesque churches.

timbers is supported from the ground by the side buttresses which become *flying buttresses* as they span the space across the aisle roof to meet the springing of the pointed vault. The *pinnacles* (small spires) act as an added weight to strengthen the points where two tensions meet.

The balance of weight and stress, as downwards pressures are met and equalized by upwards pressures, is so fine that the structure of the Gothic cathedral becomes a delicate shell enclosing the impressive interior space.

The Pazzi Chapel in the church of Santa Croce (the church of the Holy Cross) in Florence. Designed by Brunelleschi about 1430. Early Renaissance.

The balance of stresses in a Gothic Cathedral works in the same way as the two acrobats balance.

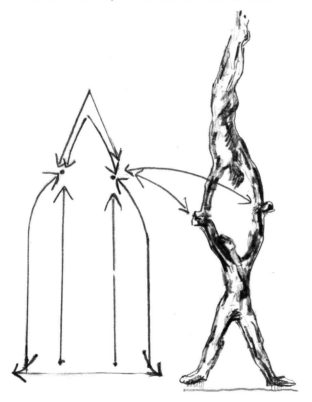

In the early years of the fifteenth century, the Renaissance architect Brunelleschi left Florence for Rome in order to make a study of the ancient Roman ruins there. He took careful measurements of the ancient remains in order to discover the rules of proportion used by Roman architects, and from these he created a new style of architecture. He did not try to copy the old Roman buildings, but adapted the old style to the needs of his day. This little chapel in Florence is not so much a monument to the glory of God as a monument to the logical mind of man. Brunelleschi related his building to the proportions of man. Unlike the Gothic architects, he had no wish to diminish man, but rather to make his buildings fit man comfortably. This chapel has the impressive dignity of ancient Roman buildings, the fantasy and complexity of the Gothic cathedral has been replaced by an ordered beauty of geometry.

This style was quickly adopted by other architects of the time; and once again the barrel vault, the dome, the classic orders (Doric, Ionic, and Corinthian columns) became features of European architecture.

In fact, the influence of Brunelleschi lasted in Europe for many hundreds of years. If you look about any Australian city you will see public buildings (such as banks, customs houses, city halls) which were built in the early years of this century, still using the features that Brunelleschi reintroduced to architecture.

It was not until the nineteenth century that new building materials encouraged new adventures in structure. This new material was iron. It was first used as a fire-resistant roofing material, but was soon being used for bridges, pavilions, galleries, market halls, and glass houses. Its use was extended to public buildings in 1843 when a library in Paris was constructed on a cast and wrought iron inner frame within a stone exterior shell. At this time the constructional iron work was usually internal and hidden from sight.

While engineers were making these first experiments in the use of iron (Machinery Hall and Eiffel Tower, pp 24, 25), European architects were involved in a situation sometimes referred to as 'the battle of the styles'. There was no distinctive 'modern' style, and architects selected from the past, swinging between Classic revival and Gothic revival. However, towards the turn of the century, a new trend known as *Art Nouveau* is discernible. This movement was a conscious attempt to break with the past, and contribute a new and unique decorative feature. Wrought iron was ideally suited to this new decoration, which consists of flowing, sinuous ornament derived from nature (the vine, the leaf, the tendril). Many of the railway stations, arcades, and kiosks built at this time make use of Art Nouveau decoration. Houses and urban buildings normally built of stone or brick could express the style in the iron-work of grills, balconies, balustrades (the 'lace' of Australian terrace houses). In Art Nouveau structures, we can see the germ of

Cast iron decoration on terrace houses in North Adelaide — repetitive decoration made possible by machine mass-production.

the modern movement, a distaste for historic ornament, and a growing appreciation of the virtue of simple forms. By the beginning of this century, steel was replacing iron as a more reliable and stronger building material. Just as the discovery of concrete opened a new field of possibility to Roman architects, so the development of steel and the reinforced concrete beam opened the way for the structure of modern architecture.

## The Structure of Twentieth Century Architecture

In any age, the most important buildings have reflected the dominant preoccupations of society at that time: the ancient Egyptians' concern with death, the Roman concern for organized power, the religious fervour of the Middle Ages, and the Renaissance concern with classical learning. Today we live in an age of technology and the machine, so it is not surprising that many of today's buildings reflect something of this in their form and structure.

We have seen how buildings of the past were enriched and enlivened by sculptured and carved surfaces; however, by the nineteenth century, machines had been made which could stamp out architectural ornament by the mile. This had nothing of the unique life of the hand-crafted detail and, as a result, architects of today have reacted against surface adornment, finding satisfaction in the simplicity of form and construction. Let us now look at some of the new methods of construction which have shaped the structures of this century.

**The reinforced concrete beam and the cantilever.** If you look at a snapped match stick you will notice that the break occurs on one side—the side away from the pressure which caused the break.

If you look at a broken twig, or any piece of wood that has snapped, you will see that the break occurs only on one side, where the wood looks as though it has been torn apart, while the other side is wrinkled, as though it has been pushed together.

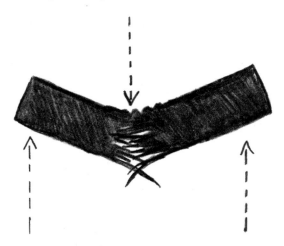

The same thing will happen to a concrete beam, therefore the steel reinforcing rod is set into the cement where the greatest stress occurs.

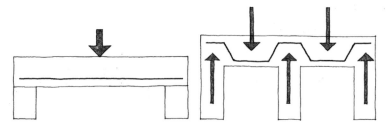

If a steel rod is inserted into a concrete beam where the greatest stress is likely to occur, the beam will be greatly strengthened. Where the concrete beam passes over supporting pillars, the stresses are reversed, and the steel rods must follow these stresses.

If the beam passes over supporting pillars, then the stress is reversed at the points where the beam receives an upward pressure from the ground. The reinforcing rod would then be set to meet and sustain these two opposing pressures. This method of strengthening concrete means that wide areas can be spanned with a horizontal beam. It also makes the *cantilever* possible. This is a suspended beam projecting into space without support from the ground. If concrete is used, then the beam is reinforced with steel rods.

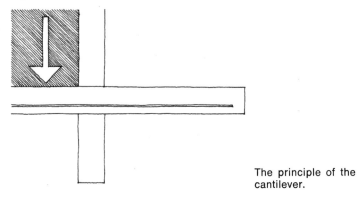

The principle of the cantilever.

Looking down into the central well of the Guggenheim Museum.

Frank Lloyd Wright (American, 1867–1959). The Solomon R. Guggenheim Museum. Designed 1943–46, built 1956–59, of reinforced concrete.

The Solomon R. Guggenheim Museum on Fifth Avenue in New York was designed by the American architect Frank Lloyd Wright, and was completed, after many years of planning, in the year that Wright died.

The seven-storey building is developed around an open well in the form of a spiral, with a huge skylight as a roof. The floors of the gallery are cantilevered out into the central well; the visitor to the gallery is taken by lift to the top of the building, and then walks down the gentle slope of the spiral reinforced concrete ramp to the ground floor. The administrative offices of the museum are in a separate spiral shaped building which is linked to the main body of the gallery by a concrete ramp.

In the photograph of the interior we see the curved floors of the main gallery (the convex curves to the right of the photograph are the balconies of an enlarged area in front of the lift well, which curves out into the central well).

Wright was trying to develop a new kind of museum in which each work of art could exist on its own without relating to the rectangular format of a normal room. However, this very aspect has been the cause of criticism—the critics claiming that the rectangular picture has evolved because of the rectangular wall, and consequently suffers against a curved surface with no horizontals to which it can relate.

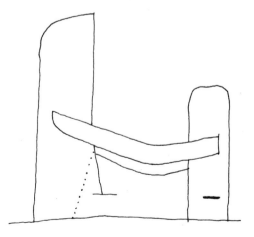

The roof of Le Corbusier's Notre Dame du Haut is a hollow shell of concrete slung between the supports of the towers and the curved wall.

103

Can you see any similarity between the neolithic dolmen and Le Corbusier's chapel?

Mies van der Rohe (German, 1886–1969). Charcoal sketch: Competition project, 1919, for a glass skyscraper on a prismatic plan, for Berlin. A perspective view showing the glass surfaces set at angles to produce a rich play of light reflections.

Le Corbusier makes use of reinforced concrete in his little chapel of Notre Dame du Haut in France. The roof is a hollow shell of concrete slung between two towers and the curved main wall. Can you notice a similar structural simplicity between the ancient prehistoric dolmen and Le Corbusier's chapel?

**The steel frame building.** Have you ever noticed how interesting buildings look while in the process of construction, when only the framework is standing? When Mies van der Rohe built his first steel and glass tower in 1950, he simply built a framework of steel and glazed it—and suddenly all the other tall buildings looked over-dressed. Van der Rohe provides the framework in which each occupant can shape his own area to his individual taste and needs. His interest is in an architecture of pure elegance of structure in which extensive use of glass gives a transparency to the building, the surface being enlivened, not by ornament or detail, but by the reflective nature of the glass.

**The use of steel cables.** By using steel cables as the skeleton of a roof structure, architects can span large areas, achieving the maximum performance from the minimum of materials.

When a cable is suspended from two points, and hangs between them, it forms a *catenary curve*. If cables of equal length are suspended between two horizontal parallel lines a simple curved surface can be obtained. If these cables are covered with wire mesh and sprayed with concrete, the roof becomes a light but tough membrane slung between parallel supports.

A catenary curve.

A surface can be generated by a series of catenary curves slung between two horizontal parallel supports.

The Australian Pavilion at Osaka in Japan was designed by James McCormick for Expo 70. The giant cantilevered building rises to a height of 39 metres (as high as a ten-storey building) and curves over to form a 'sky-hook'. Housed on four floors inside the cantilevered building are administrative offices, reception, and

104

James McCormick (Australian). The Australian Pavilion for Expo 70, at Osaka, Japan. Steel and sprayed concrete. (Steel cable construction).

Yunken, Freeman Brothers, Griffiths & Simpson. The Sidney Myer Music Bowl, Melbourne, 1959. Aluminium sheathed plywood supported on steel cables.

dining rooms. From the sky-hook is suspended a circular free-hanging roof, 48.8 metres in diameter. This roof is constructed on a web of suspension cables, and provided shelter for visitors as they queued at the pavilion entrance. The pavilion is built of steel and sprayed concrete.

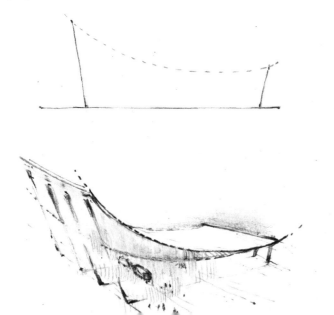

By the use of steel cables, either under tension or suspensed in a catenary curve, architects can now span large areas—such as park pavilions, exhibition halls, and music bowls.

Moshe Safdie's Habitat (page 32) is built in an earthquake zone, and has been designed to withstand a severe earthquake. All units are tied together with high tensile rods and cables (rather like those toys which have elastic running through them; when the elastic is taut the toys stand upright, but they collapse if the tension at the base is released). Rubber strips between the units act as a dampener (like shock absorbers in a car) to any movement caused by earthquake. The strength of the structure is therefore not in its rigidity, but in its flexibility.

**The dome.** Modern technology has produced materials tough enough and light enough to enclose large areas without the problem of supporting a colossal weight of stone or concrete. The same principle that keeps the silk of the parachute in a state of tension, works with modern spans—a balance between internal and external air pressures.

105

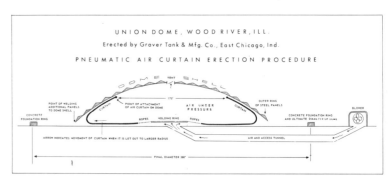

Buckminster Fuller (American, *b.* 1895). The geodesic dome for the Union Tank Car Company at Wood River, Illinois, under construction, showing the inflated balloon.

Thin 'skins' of concrete, plastic, or alloy can now be stretched across reinforcing girders or cables enclosing the largest amount of space with the least amount of material. When you think of the enormous weight of concrete in the dome of the Pantheon, and the elaborate engineering of the foundations, walls, and buttresses which supported this weight, you can realize the advantages of these new light materials.

In 1953 the Union Tank Car Company commissioned Buckminster Fuller to design a dome in which many tankers could be serviced simultaneously (see page 32). This dome spans 117 metres without internal support (at the time it was built it was the largest dome in the world, being twenty three times the volume of St Peter's dome in Rome). The dome is built of hexagonal panels of steel, braced externally with steel tubes and rods bolted together. The steel of the panels is only just over 3 millimetres thick, which in proportion to the span is considerably thinner than an egg shell. This dome was constructed from the ground circumference with cranes working inside lifting the panels into position. However,

when he built a second dome for the same company, the architect had this one erected by pneumatic cushion lift. An enormous balloon was placed under the central panels, and, as the balloon was slowly inflated, panels were added to the lower edges until the dome was completed. This meant that construction of the dome started at the top and all the building took place at ground level without the use of cranes or scaffolding.

Buckminster Fuller has said: "The achievement of the good life for one man depends on the realization of the good life for every man". He has prepared an inventory of all the materials in the world, and by relating this to the number of people in the world, he can find out how much we can each have without being greedy. The need to find solutions to modern problems of crowded urban development—to house as many people as economically as possible—has been modern architects' chief concern. The best solutions have been those in which the architects have made use of modern technology without losing sight of the basic needs of man—both his physical and his imaginative needs.

# chapter 7

# STRUCTURE IN PAINTING

In the previous chapter we discussed the structure of buildings, observing how man has developed new methods of building in order to satisfy different needs. If you look around the room you are sitting in, it is not too difficult to see how the architect or builder has arranged the space of the room. However, it is not always so easy to see how a painter 'builds' his picture. Just as a building is made up of many parts which together make the whole, so a painter organizes each part of his picture so that his intention or aim can become real and meaningful. The structure can be extremely simple or highly complex, making the picture either tense and dynamic, or still and tranquil; but it must have that sense of 'oneness' in which each part contributes in some way to the total impact of the picture. By this, I do not mean that a picture must be perfectly balanced and logical, for the artist's aim may be to produce an image of an illogical and unexpected nature. However, he must still structure the parts so that they convey this intention in the most forceful way possible.

An Etruscan artist painted this picture on the walls of an underground tomb in the fifth century B.C., some twenty years before the temple of the Parthenon was started in Athens. The Etruscans created the most important civilization in Italy before the Romans; in their properous days (from 700 B.C. to 575 B.C.) they controlled most of central Italy to the north of the Greek colonies.

*The Flute Player, c.* 470 B.C. Fresco from the Tomb of the Leopards, an Etruscan necropolis at Tarquinia.

Haunted by the fear of death and the fate awaiting them in the after-life, the Etruscans developed a funerary art whose aim was to perpetuate the joyful aspects of life in order to counteract the fear of a dark and unknown underworld.

In this painting we see a musician with a double flute walking through a garden towards the banqueting hall. The artist is more concerned with finding the right shapes and lines to express *internal* feelings and energies than in describing accurately how the figure looked from the outside.

For instance, if you close your eyes, then stretch your fingers tautly into a flute-playing position, and concentrate hard on the *internal sensation,* you will probably feel your fingers grow large, like the fingers in the Etruscan mural. Notice how the lines and colours of the musician's tunic and cape suggest the forceful stride of the man as he moves briskly past the delicate trees of the garden. D. H. Lawrence writes of these Etruscan murals: "The curves of their limbs show pleasure in life, a pleasure that goes deeper still in the limbs of the dancers, in the big, long hands thrown out and dancing to the very ends of the fingers, a dance that surges from within, like a current in the sea. It is as if the current of some strong, different life swept through them, different from our shallow current today; as if they drew their vitality from different depths that we are denied."

Whereas the history of architecture is closely linked to the development of man's technology, the same tendency is not so evident in the history of painting. The materials that man has used through the ages—mosaic, fresco, oil, and now acrylic, have to some extent influenced the end result. However, the manner in which he has manipulated his medium in order to give life to his idea has not radically changed. This picture by Picasso was painted more than 2400 years after the Etruscan wall painting, and yet there are certain elements which closely link it with the earlier painting. Picasso is using colour and shape to communicate *an internal sensation and reality*.

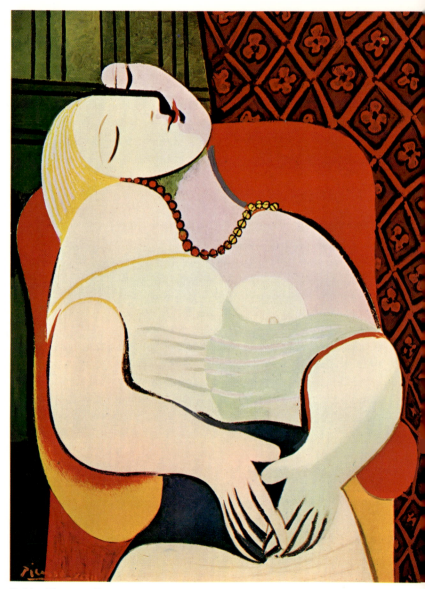

Pablo Picasso (Spanish, 1881–1973). *The Dream*, 1932. Collection of Victor W. Ganz, New York.

Jan van Eyck (Flemish, 1385–1441). *The Marriage of Jan Arnolfini and His Wife*, 1434. Oil and tempera on a wooden panel. 77 x 53 cms. London, The National Gallery.

Leonardo da Vinci (Italian, 1452–1519) *Mona Lisa, c.* 1500–04. Oil and tempera on a wooden panel, 77 x 53 cms. Paris, The Louvre.

The face floats weightlessly on the warm curve of the shoulder —you can see two faces simultaneously. The pale yellow profile lies dreaming heavily within the shape of the full face. The full face smiles as if dreaming just below the surface of consciousness, but the profile face is deeper in sleep and totally relaxed. The arms weigh heavily and the fingertips touch in such a way that we feel the sleeper is still vaguely conscious of the contact. By painting one arm pink and the other warm green Picasso suggests not only the shadow side of the figure, but also that strange feeling of detachment that sometimes comes when we remain conscious of our limbs in sleep; they seem miles apart and yet they touch. This soft, dreaming form is held in by the positive red of the armchair and the dense-patterned background.

Just as the Etruscan painter of the fifth century B.C. distorts the shape of his figure in order to give added richness to his idea, so the Spanish painter of the twentieth century distorts the shape and colour of his sleeping woman in order to give a much richer experience of sleep.

You will remember that Jan van Eyck's aim was to produce a sensation of real space, and to make a precise record of his vision. However, like Picasso and the Etruscan artist, van Eyck realized that the impact of his picture relied on its structure—in the fusion of parts into one image. The picture can be divided into two parts: 'his' and 'hers'. 'His' side is more austere in shape and colour, 'hers' softer in shape and richer in colour. Compare the vertical lines of the window with the soft red curtains of the bed; the vertical lines of his dark cloak, with the soft and heavy fall of her green velvet gown. However, these two parts are cleverly linked and made one by the joined hands, by the small dog at their feet, and by the curve of the candelabra which repeats the curve of their linked hands. Imagine the picture without that round mirror on the wall; the space between the figures then becomes a void. Van Eyck has used many symbols (which would have needed no explanation at the time) in order to give his picture added significance. The single lighted candle symbolizes purity; the dog, fidelity; and the fruit on the window sill and chest, fruitfulness. As with all great painting, there is far more to be seen than is apparent at first glance.

We have already discussed this picture by Leonardo da Vinci, noticing how he creates an illusion of volumes in space by the use of delicately modulated lights and shades. Now we must see how he structures the parts in order to make such an arresting image.

The basic structure is a very simple one—a stable triangle superimposed against a series of horizontals. However, a close study reveals much more. If you block out the left hand side of the picture with a piece of paper, and look only at the right side, you will notice that the forms at the corner of the eye and mouth pull upwards; the cloak across the shoulder pushes up; the horizontal lines of the landscape culminate in misty mountain peaks. Now block out the right side—this upward tension seems to relax; the forms of the face have less upward pull and the landscape seems to be moving down rather than up (your eye moving down the curved mountain road). When you look again at the complete picture, you can notice that the horizon line on the right side of the figure is actually higher than the horizon on the left. Why did Leonardo do this? Certainly, it is no accident, for Leonardo da Vinci's mind was always in control of any situation. The tension created between these two opposing forces (one up and one down), held in such delicate balance as to be almost unnoticeable, is part of the vitality of the picture.

We have already seen that the painters and architects of the Renaissance era became interested in the ordered beauty of geometry. This picture by Piero della Francesca was painted about 1450, some sixteen years after van Eyck painted the portrait group of Jan Arnolfini and his wife.

Piero has painted his picture on a wooden panel cut to the proportions of the *golden mean,* or the *golden section* (where the relation between the width and length of a rectangle is 1 : 1.618, that is, approximately 8 : 13, which was used by the ancient Greeks to achieve, what was to them, the ideally proportioned rectangle). You will notice that the group of small figures depicting Pontius Pilate witnessing the flagellation of Christ makes another rectangle, identically proportioned to the whole picture. The larger group of three standing figures on the right form yet another rectangle (but in this case, not a golden mean rectangle). The vanishing point of all perspective lines (marked cᴜ the diagram)

Piero della Francesca (Italian, 1410/20–1492). *The Flagellation of Christ.* Signed. Panel, 59 x 81.5 cms. Urbino, Palazzo Ducale.

is just off centre in the lower half of the picture, attracting your eye into the centre and forming an unconscious tie, linking the separate geometric parts. Notice that the direction of the dark diagonal of the ceiling beam directs your eye down to the head of Christ. Place a piece of tracing paper over this reproduction and, ignoring the figures, trace out the numerous squares and rectangles marked out by the groups of figures and architectural features. You will then discover that, as well as being a realistic picture of objects in space, bathed in the clear light of early morning, this is also a piece of intricate abstract geometry. In fact, Piero della Francesca's interest in geometry was so great that he later stopped painting and concentrated all his energies on setting down his theories of mathematical proportions.

Piet Mondrian (Dutch, 1872–1944). *The Grey Tree,* 1912. 78.5 x 107.5 cms. Collection, Haags Gemeentemuseum, The Hague.

The twentieth century Dutch painter Piet Mondrian, like Piero della Francesca, was interested in the geometry of space and colour. In the painting reproduced here, *The Grey Tree,* we can see him giving shape to the growth-energy and structure of the tree, in terms of arcs and curved lines which push up or fold back on themselves, enclosing spaces—spaces which take on the nature of a cellular growth; concentrated and intense in the centre, but becoming more loosely held together as they move out to the outer edges of the tree.

From the horizontal of the ground a powerful energy moves up in a strong vertical curve which supports the forms which extend and expand into space.

Mondrian's later paintings became abstract, although still concerned with the stretch of lines which enclose spaces and areas of colour. He spoke of "expansion and limitation" (extreme opposites) as "the creative factors of space".

He once said "Impressed by the vastness of nature, I was trying to express its expansion, rest and unity. At the same time, I was fully aware that the visible expansion of nature is its limitation [the limitation of human vision and understanding]; vertical and horizontal lines are the expression of two opposing forces; these exist everywhere; their reciprocal action constitutes 'life'."

These vertical and horizontal lines became the life force of his later abstract paintings—the white, black, or grey rectangles and squares enclosed by these lines becoming space; the red, yellow, and blue areas becoming form. However, it was the stretch and pull of opposing forces that interested him. At an exhibition of his paintings he was once asked why he always painted squares, to which he replied, "Squares, Madam? I see no squares."

It is interesting to remember that Mondrian came from the flat landscape of Holland—a land of horizontals and verticals, of closely cultivated fields enclosed by dykes, a land in which man's survival depends on an imposed geometry and order.

In El Greco's *Cleansing of the Temple* the calm and static beauty of Piero della Francesca's geometry gives way to turbulent movement and surface tension. Much of the tension of the painting relies on opposing directions which cut across the surface of the picture (see diagram). With a ruler test these directions for yourself, and perhaps find others which tie movement or gestures together across the picture plane. You will notice that El Greco isolates the figure of Christ by using a sharp pink which creates an acid discord with the dense yellow of the robe immediately to the left. These two colours float forward from the closely harmonized, muted colours on either side.

El Greco (Greek, 1541–1614). *The Cleansing of the Temple*. London, The National Gallery. The structure of the painting.

The modern American artist Jackson Pollock is also concerned with activating the surface of his canvas with dynamic movement and energies. However, in this case he uses abstraction—the energies are not created by the direction of limbs or drapery but by the direction of lines of paint. These directions are built up in thick layers, so that the texture of paint becomes an important aspect of the work. Pollock worked on very large canvases which he laid flat on the studio floor. Many of the lines in his composition are a description of the actual physical energy involved in their making (the swing of his arm, or the movement of his whole body as he moves across the large canvas). His aim was to allow the painting to form as spontaneously as possible, controlling the movement instinctively rather than intellectually. However, his satisfaction of the end result depended on the degree of energy and life the picture generated. This method of painting—sometimes

called *Action* painting—produced a spate of 'trick' paintings: riding bicycles across the canvas and putting loaded paint brushes into the hands of apes. However, without the control of real sensibility, the result of these exercises was merely so much paint on canvas, whereas the surface of a Pollock painting can be as exciting as the surface of an El Greco or a Tintoretto.

Jackson Pollock (American, 1912–1956). *The She-Wolf,* 1943. Collection of the Museum of Modern Art, New York.

113

Cézanne (French, 1839–1906). *Portrait of Ambroise Vollard,* 1899. The structural lines which hold the major areas together add to our experience of the picture plane.

Cézanne builds the form of his picture with *colour*. He creates a feeling of depth by diminishing the energies of the colours as they move back into the picture. When I mention the *energy* of colour, I mean the way some colours seem to bounce boldly forward towards your eye, while others sit quietly back. Try putting a stroke of brilliant orange-red next to a blue-grey and notice which one has more forward bounce or energy. Now look at the orange of the near roofs in Cézanne's landscape, and compare this with the pinks and muted oranges of the background.

Paul Cézanne French, 1839–1906). *Mont Sainte Victoire,* 1904–06. Oil on canvas, 73.3 x 92.1 cms. The Philadelphia Museum of Art. George W. Elkins Collection.

Leonardo da Vinci created a sensation of depth by contrasting the dark shape of Mona Lisa with the light misty greys of the background. This is a contrast of light and dark—a tonal contrast. However, Cézanne uses very little tonal contrast. The space in his picture is made by contrasts of colour. The whole surface of the canvas seems to vibrate with light, and planes of colour float before our eyes as sensations of warm and cool areas, rather than as clearly defined objects. This picture was painted between 1904 and 1906. Many people found it difficult to understand this new

attitude to colour, as had the people of the nineteenth century the fresh greenness of a Constable landscape.

Cézanne's contemporary, the French painter Claude Monet, also used colour to structure his pictures. He realized that colour is light, and that the colour of any object depends upon the quality and strength of light which bounces off it. For example, a tree can appear vivid green in the clear, uninterrupted light of midday, yet a smoky blue in the misty light of early morning, and have no colour at all in the middle of the night. We cannot say with finality

Claude Monet, (French, 1840–1926). *Gare St-Lazare* (The St-Lazare railway station in Paris), 1877. Paris, Jeu de Paume.

**115**

that the tree is green, only that it appears green in certain lights. Monet's desire was to make his paint take on the vitality and bounce of light itself. He set up his palette only with the colours of the spectrum (the colours of light), using no browns, ochres, or blacks. He realized that shadows are not an absence of light but merely light of a different quality. So instead of making his shadow areas negative darks, they become glowing colours of less intensity and bounce than the light areas.

It was this interest in the transformation of objects brought about by different light conditions that led Monet to paint the same subject again and again. He painted a series of the front of Rouen Cathedral. In one, the vast complicated facade melts in pink and blue mists; in another it is veiled in the gold haze of midday, seen against the dense blue of the sky. He painted ten paintings of the Gare St Lazare; the one reproduced here transforms the grimy railway station into a sensation of vibrant light filtering through a screen of steam and smoke. The warm light bouncing off the distant buildings of Paris just manages to filter through the smoke, so that the buildings lose all sense of gravity and volume and float in our vision as colour sensations. The denser smoke from the train in the centre is blocking out more light, sifting out the warmth, and producing a sensation of cool blues and mauves. If you let your eye move across the surface of this picture (from edge to edge) you will notice that every area is alive. These are no dark 'holes' of space, or negative areas—each part is a positive sensation of colour, which we can translate into a sensation of objects in space.

Five years before Monet painted this picture of the railway station, he had exhibited a painting called *Impressions: Sunrise*. It was this picture that caused a critic of the day to call Monet, and other French painters with a similar interest in colour, *Impressionists*. The critic's intention was to mock these young painters for disregarding established traditions in painting, but the term stuck, and *Impressionists* they have been ever since.

Georges Seurat, a French contemporary of Cézanne and Monet, painted this picture of *Bathers at Asnieres* in 1883. He took Monet's theory of colour even further—by breaking up areas of colour into tiny dots of pure colour, he hoped to produce a more vital surface of colour; colour which would more closely resemble the sensation of light. For example, the green of the grassy bank is made up of points of pure yellow, blue, yellow-green, mauve, blue-green—which all together produce the desired sensation of 'green'.

This method of using colour has been termed *pointillism* or sometimes *divisionism*. However, even more interesting in the work of Seurat is his obsessive concern with pictorial order. The shapes of this painting have the same feeling of absolute 'rightness' that we have already seen in the work of Piero della Francesca. The play of curves against diagonals, and of verticals against horizontals have the same satisfying geometry of a Piero or a Mondrian.

The revolutionary attitude towards colour which we have seen in the works of the French painters of the nineteenth century was to have a profound influence on many of the painters of this century. The early Byzantine, Romanesque, and Gothic painters of Europe had realized the power of colour in communicating an idea. However, Renaissance artists, in their desire to achieve an actual sensation of volumes in space, had resorted to *tone* (contrasts of light and dark). Of course they used colour, but seldom as the major structure of the picture.

When we see Picasso using a green shadow under the sleeper's chin in *The Dream*, and a blue line to separate the neck from the armchair, or a red line to separate the arm from the blouse, we realize that colour is no longer being used merely to describe an object (a blue sky or a red apple) but is now used as dominant or recessive energies which create the structure and life of the picture.

Georges Seurat (French, 1859–1891). *Bathers at Asnières,* 1883–84. London, The National Gallery.

117

Colin Lanceley (Australian, *b.* New Zealand, 1938). *Monsoon II,* 1969. Oil on wood and canvas, 185.4 cms square. Collection of Kym Bonython.

In *Monsoon II,* Australian painter Colin Lanceley breaks with the traditional idea that a painting must be a flat rectangle upon which one creates illusions with colour. (English painter David Hockney also dispenses with the rectangular canvas: see page 82.) Lanceley's painting is neither flat nor rectangular. On an undulating diamond shape he creates a series of explosive situations both with paint and with projecting painted objects. The coloured tubes become a linear energy, and loop around the canvas, suggesting an equally active surface hidden from our view. The shapes and colours seem to grow on the white surface, spontaneous and buoyant as brightly coloured flowers.

In some recent Australian paintings we can see an interest in colour structure resulting from the discoveries and inventions of the European colourists of the nineteenth and twentieth centuries.

Roy Churcher (Australian,
*b*. England 1933). *Entrance*, 1972.
Acrylic on canvas. Collection of
Mrs Beverley Wright.

In this picture by Brisbane artist Roy Churcher, we look down a hallway to a pot of geraniums standing on the balcony. The painter is not concerned with recording the factual details of the visual experience, but rather in using colour to translate a sensation of light—so that the colours relive the immediate joy of the initial sensation (that first experience, when we *feel* the colours more than we *see* them in an analytical way). For example, the pot of geraniums has such energy and life that the red seems to float forward, contradicting its position in space. The circle of yellow that floats above, is the bounce of light on a yellow tree outside, and, in the hallway, a mat which absorbs the light instead of reflecting it, becomes a dense purple—the colour not describing the actual colour of the mat, but rather its density in the context of the total experience. The structure of the painting is therefore a structure of colour, in which each part has an individual existence, yet together they become a single sensation.

119

Mervyn Moriarty (Australian, *b.* 1937). *A Place to Listen.* Acrylic on canvas. Collection of the artist.

Mervyn Moriarty, another painter from Brisbane, also uses colour to structure his pictures. The painting reproduced here, *A Place to Listen,* is one of a group of pictures that the artist painted in which he breaks up large areas with bands of extraordinarily subtle colour changes.

The visual stimulus that gave rise to these paintings occurred while driving along a flat road, past groups of trees, with the water of Moreton Bay behind. Moriarty noticed the broken flash of light that cut between the trunks of the trees; the steady intensity of light that came with every break, then fragmentation again as the car moved past more trees. His aim was to transpose a similar sensation to a still thing—his painting. He does not want to give a sensation of movement, but rather to create a situation in which no area is fixed and positive; a situation in which spaces can be rearranged and readjusted as we look at the picture. You will notice that no part is so positive that it cannot be interchanged, and become part of another area. Like the fragmented view seen from a moving car, our eye moves across bands of colour, weaving through from one part to another, yet always with a sense of a total image—a logical structure behind the fragmentation.

Here are five more recent Australian paintings. Can you see how the artists have organized and structured their pictures in order to communicate their ideas? Decide first what the artist is trying to do, then see if you can discover the means he has used in order to create a forceful and unified image.

Jan Senbergs (Australian, *b.* Latvia, 1939). *Column and Still Objects,* 1968. Acrylic and screenprint on canvas, 167.6 x 213.4 cms. Rudy Komon Art Gallery.

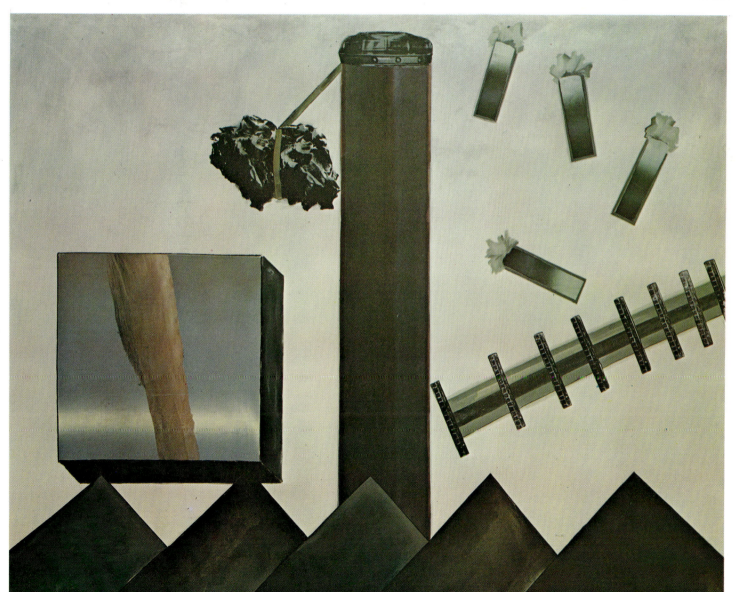

John Brack (Australian, *b.* 1920). *Portrait of Dr Hattam,* 1965. Oil on canvas, 115.6 x 81.3 cms. Collection of Mrs V. Macallister.

Sam Fullbrook (Australian, *b.* 1922). *Portrait of Jim Wigley,* 1965. Oil on canvas, 101.6 x 76.2 cms. Canberra, National Collection.

William Rose (Australian, b. 1930). *Flight Number 1,* 1968. Oil on hardboard, 152.4 x 243.8 cms. Bonython Art Gallery.

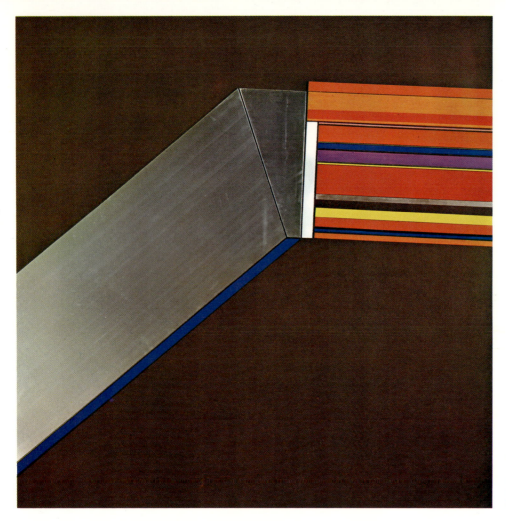

Nevil Matthews (Australian, *b.* 1930).
*Three Intervals Number 3*, 1969. Wood,
acrylic, and aluminium on board, 172.7
cms square. Collection of
Mimosa Fay Matthews.

This chapter has dealt with the many different ways a painter can 'build' his picture, the structure and form depending a great deal on the idea being communicated. It is important to realize that this structuring is a conscious intention on the part of the artist and not the result of a 'happy accident'. If you look back to most of the reproductions in this chapter you will notice that each part of the picture holds its own individuality, but all the parts together become a single image. Thomas Aquinas once defined the properties of beauty as "harmony, unity, and radiance". Harmony is the relation of parts to the whole, unity is the single image, radiance is the ability to project that image—so that its life and vitality can radiate out to the observer. If a person possesses the first two qualities, but lacks the third—that is, the personality to radiate the harmony and unity of form, then that person falls short of true beauty. In the same way, a painting must have the 'personality' to project the quality of its structure.

# chapter 8

# STRUCTURE AND FORM
# IN SCULPTURE

This clay bison was modelled by a palaeolithic cave dweller some time between 13 000 and 10 000 B.C. The cave man who shaped this bison into existence was performing the magic act of creation; by pulling the likeness of a bison out of a shapeless lump of clay, he possesses it, and makes it his own. This desire to possess through the act of forming motivates artists now, as it did in those early years of man's history. However, to palaeolithic man the created image worked a more potent magic; not only did man gain power over the beast through his ability to recreate, but the replica image ensured the continuance of the animals so necessary to man's existence.

It is interesting to notice that man's visual perception was as sharp then as it is now. Notice how he has modelled the shoulders of the bison so that you can feel the pent up energy and power of the animal, the alert tension of the head, the wild eye and flaring nostril.

*Bison, c.* 13 000 B.C. Modelled in clay on a mound of rock in the Tuc d'Audobert cave in Southern France, during the Palaeolithic period (*c.* 35 000 B.C.–*c.* 10 000 B.C.). 61 cms long.

*Peasant Guiding a Plough.* Egyptian, *c.* 2000 B.C. London, The British Museum.

This little clay model of a peasant guiding a plough was made by an Egyptian craftsman about 2000 B.C.—at least 8000 years after the bison was modelled. The wild eyed, untamed bison has become a docile, spotted oxen obediently pulling a plough for man. Just as man has tamed and ordered his environment, so to a certain extent he has tamed and ordered his means of expression. If you look at these two works together, you will notice that the palaeolithic man has put all his energy into recreating the actuality of the animal—its spirit and life as well as its appearance. But there is no attempt to make the bison part of an ordered scene or idea. However, the Egyptian artist, being part of an organized society, is more a detached observer, recording in clay a little incident from everyday life. The forms have become a more simplified sign language because the written word and the visual image are now a means of communication. The ancient cave man was not yet interested in communicating an idea; instead he was performing a magic and secret rite of creation.

If primitive man had the ability to produce works of such startling realism as the *Bison,* it follows that simplified forms and stylized forms (which have been used at different times in history, both in the past and today) are not the result of an inability to produce a work of realism, but rather the result of a different need or a different attitude to the work being produced.

For instance, this small marble statuette of a lyre player, found on a little island in the Aegean Sea, was made about the same time as the Egyptian ploughman, yet the aim of the artist was quite different. In this work we feel that the artist is coaxing the smooth, fine-textured marble in order to produce the utmost tactile sensaion. The smooth shapes loop and turn, merge and separate, giving a

*Lyre Player.* Cycladic, *c.* 2000 B.C. Athens, The National Archaeological Museum.

sensation of a continuous unbroken movement. One can imagine the pleasure the artist felt as he ran his hands across the smooth stylized upturned face, then down the curve of the chair to the loops that make the legs of the chair. This work is only 17.8 centimetres high, so could be held in the hand and appreciated as a tactile object. In this sense it is a much more sophisticated work than the highly realistic paleolithic bison, in that the artist is using shape, line, and texture in an abstract manner to stimulate our senses and give pleasure to our eyes in the same way that music gives pleasure to our ears.

The Aegean culture which produced the little *Lyre Player* culminated in the work of classical Greek art in the fifth century B.C.—a brief moment in history when man seemed to find the perfect balance between mind and matter. By this I mean that the sculptured shapes express both the philosophy of the time (their belief in an ideal state) and also the Greeks' awareness and love of the natural world.

The fragment reproduced here comes from the parapet of a small temple dedicated to Athena Nike (Victory) at the entrance to the Acropolis. It is one of a series of Victories preparing a sacrifice. This one is removing her sandals before entering the sacred enclosure. Some elements of the earlier *Lyre Player* remain—the quality of finely 'drawn' marble and the sensuous tactile quality. However, in this work there is a more delicate balance between the idea (the fluid rhythm of a gesture caught in mid-action) and the physical actuality of the woman's body. Notice how the drapery flows like rivulets of water from her left shoulder and down from the raised knee. Our eyes are pulled towards the hand that loosens the sandal strap, but there is a counter-tension in the pull of drapery over the broken arm which once balanced the figure. Although this relief was originally placed well above eye level, it is as finely and as delicately drawn as the most fragile detail in nature.

*Nike Untying Her Sandal*. Classical Greek, *c*. 410–407 B.C. Marble, about 142 cms high. Athens, Acropolis Museum.

You will remember that Christianity made new expressive demands on painters and sculptors—a simple sign language was developed in which symbols and signs played an important role in communicating the religious idea. Romanesque sculpture was used both to tell the religious story and to enliven and give emphasis to significant parts of the architectural structure—particularly the doorways. If it lacks the grace and elegance of Greek sculpture, it yet has its own vitality—the vitality of a blunt and forthright language.

The *Eve of Autun* originally formed part of the lintel of a church door. As the carving ran across the top of the doorway, the sculptor was obliged to arrange the figure horizontally. However, he has exploited this restriction by creating an Eve of exceptional charm. She floats as if in a dream, through lush and sinuous vegetation, plucking the fruit with her left hand as she turns towards Adam.

*Eve with the Forbidden Fruit.* Romanesque, 1120–1135. Low relief. Musée Rolin, Autun.

If you compare this Romanesque carving with the Greek carving of *Nike Removing Her Sandal,* you will notice a different attitude to the human body. The Greeks did not make a 'sin' of life, and the body was glorified as a symbol of structural perfection. Now, although the Romanesque *Eve* has a certain sensual charm, we are yet aware of a degree of shyness on the part of the artist in representing her nudity. Throughout the Romanesque period people's thoughts were preoccupied with the horrors of hell and damnation, and many things of this world were regarded with the gravest suspicion—lest they lead to temptation and ultimate damnation. However, during the thirteenth century a new attitude to religion grew—a religion based on the all-embracing love of God, in contrast with the wrathful, vengeful God of Romanesque times. Creation and all its creatures were sanctified by this new concept of a God of Love. The figures of Gothic cathedrals take on a new life and reality, and the ornamentation of the cathedrals flowers with details from nature—ivy, grape, holly, lily—the monsters that adorned the Romanesque capitals are pushed out by delicate leaves and flowers, and only appear as *gargoyles* (carved water spouts) spitting out rainwater from the roof of the cathedral.

Once again we see the changing attitudes and thoughts of man influencing the things he makes.

This new interest and love for the things of nature continued into the next era—the Renaissance. However, because of the interest in classical art, Renaissance man was searching for an *ideal*—and was therefore more concerned with finding the right form to embody an idea or concept than in depicting nature with the simple directness of the Gothic artist. Michelangelo was only twenty three years old when he carved the *Pietà*. He aimed at *perfection of form* to symbolize the perfection of the Virgin Mary's submission to the divine will. You will notice that Michelangelo organized the group into a firmly built pyramid—yet within that simple structure, lines and forms cut diagonally, creating a dynamic tension within the simple overall shape. When Michelangelo was once asked to define

Michelangelo Buonarroti (Italian, 1475–1564). *Pietà,* 1498–99. Marble. In St Peter's Cathedral, Rome.

Henry Moore (English, *b.* 1898). *Three Piece Reclining Figure,* 1961-62. Bronze, 2.9 metres long. Collection, The Bank of Canada, Montreal.

the attributes of a great piece of sculpture, he replied that it should be possible to roll it down a hill without damage! In spite of his obvious impatience at such a question, his answer does convey one of his firm beliefs—that the dynamics of the work should be held firmly in, and something of the solid grandeur of the uncut marble block should remain.

The English sculptor Henry Moore made this large *Reclining Figure* in 1961. It was made first in plaster then cast in bronze. Coming straight after the finely worked *Pietà* of Michelangelo, it is something of a shock to be thrust so suddenly into the twentieth century. However, there are elements of similarity between the two. Like Michelangelo, Moore has great respect for the material he uses—he allows the nature of the wood, marble, sandstone, or plaster to determine to a certain extent the final result. Like Michelangelo, all his work adheres to two strong sculptural values—those of volume and surface tension. (The push of forms, held tautly in by the surface.) Like Michelangelo, Moore is searching for an archetypal form. Their concept of the ideal form is, of course,

quite different. In Michelangelo's early work, he was searching for the ideal of beauty. Moore's ideal is more the ideal of vitality—the nature of all organic things that have been structured by growth. He has said: "There are universal shapes to which everyone is subconsciously conditioned, and to which we can respond *if our conscious control does not shut them off.*"

Although the work reproduced here was inspired by the monumental structure of the human body, the forms also evoke other natural forms—for instance, there are elements of a rugged landscape of cliffs and valleys; there is something of the water-worn river pebble, or the smooth curves and projections of bones. Moore's eye is constantly searching for the forms and structures of nature. He has said of a walk along the sea shore: "Out of the millions of pebbles passed, I choose but to see with excitement only those which fit in with my *existing* form interest at the time. A different thing happens if I sit down and examine a handful one by one. I may extend my form-experience more, by giving my mind *time* to *become conditioned* to a *new shape*."

Picasso has enjoyed using his ingenuity and wit to create a form of sculpture that has become an important development in twentieth century sculpture—the ready-made and junk sculpture (see Klippel, page 80). Picasso's delightful visual pun, reproduced here, has been made from a series of 'found' objects. The body is a basket

Pablo Picasso (Spanish, 1881–1973). *Baboon and Young,* 1951. Bronze, 53.3 cms high. Collection, The Museum of Modern Art, The Mrs Simon Guggenheim Fund.

ball; the head of the baboon: two toy cars that belonged to his small son; the baboon's ears: the broken handles of a china jug found in a dump. These, with other found objects, have been welded together with plaster and later cast in bronze.

Marcel Duchamp, a French artist of this century, was the first artist to use the 'ready-made' as an alternative to the already accepted notion of structure and form. Duchamp belonged to a movement called *Dada,* which started in Zurich at the outbreak of the First World War. This movement deliberately set about trying to shock people into reassessing their code of values—that is, the existing values of a society which had permitted this war to happen. Amongst these men was a very real desire for freedom—freedom of thought and freedom of action. They experimented with well established thoughts and well known objects—turning the familiar on its head, placing it out of context, mocking it—in order to find out if the well known 'here' was not hiding an unfamiliar and wonderful 'there'. To the Dadaist, "Life is not here alone, but also there, there, there" (in German, da, da, da).

Although the German words for "there, there" ("da, da"), may explain the origin of the word Dada, its specific meaning is a mystery—intentionally so. The Dadaists, who set themselves against the logical and the familiar, may have chosen a name for themselves which had no significance at all. However, by never feeling the need to explain themselves, the Dadaists compel us to approach their work with a puzzled mind, a mind unable to form any premature opinions.

In art, Dadaism became a movement of *Anti-Art*—a desire to shock or baffle the complacent gallery goer into rethinking and reassessing.

Duchamp made a positive gesture towards anti-art when in 1917 he submitted for exhibition at the first New York Salon des Independents a urinal entitled *Fountain* and signed by 'R. Mutt' (the name of a firm of sanitary engineers). The selection committee indignantly rejected this "shameless article". Some contended that

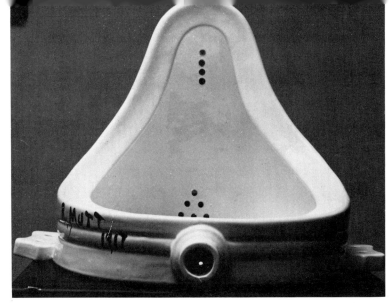

Marcel Duchamp (French, 1887–1968). *Fountain,* 1917. Ready-made, 60 cms high. Milan, Galleria Schwarz.

Mr Mutt's *Fountain* was immoral and vulgar; others, that it was not a work of art, but merely a plain piece of plumbing. As to the first complaint, it is no more immoral than a bath tub, being a fixture that can be seen everyday in plumbers' show windows. The second complaint—that it only qualifies as a work of art if made by Mr Mutt's own hands—was considered unimportant by Duchamp and other New York Dadaists. Duchamp stated that what was important was that the artist *chose* it (just as Monet chose a railway station). The artist took an ordinary article of life, then presented it in such a way that its usefulness was no longer significant, and, under a new title, in a new situation, created a new *thought* for that object.

If you think about this, this same attitude could apply to any work of art. The artist is selecting and then presenting his selection in a memorable way, so that it takes on new life and meaning for us. To Michelangelo, the idea or concept was the significant aspect of the work—the detailed execution was seldom carried out 'by his own hand' but often was left to skilled stonemasons working under Michelangelo's direction.

To make this point clear, Duchamp later exhibited an ordinary wooden hat rack (a circular base that screwed to the under side of a shelf, with six curved pegs for coats or hats). He presented it by suspending it from the ceiling of the gallery on an invisible thread. By isolating the object, and removing it from its normal function, he draws our attention, and we look at it as a shape, floating mysteriously in space. However, at another exhibition, he had the same object screwed to a shelf near the door, and visitors to the gallery (some of whom had previously admired it as a work of art) failed to recognize it, and hung their coats on it without a second glance. Duchamp was showing us that the most ordinary object can become extraordinary through the eye of the artist, and through the manner of its presentation. He was shocking us into looking.

A sketch of Duchamp's *Hat Rack.*

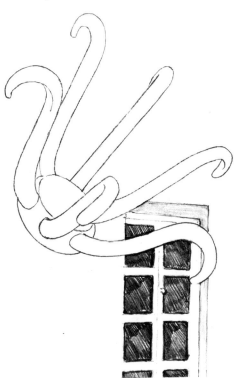

131

Although Duchamp threw these 'ready-mades' in the public's eye as a challenge, never intending the idea to be adopted as an acceptable art form, the idea had nevertheless sown the seeds for the *Pop* movement of the 1960s. Dada in fact gave painting and sculpture a new lease of life, in that it opened the doors to an 'anything goes' freedom of materials and subject matter.

When the American Christo came out to Sydney to 'wrap up' Little Bay, he was giving shape to a concept that had no permanence and could not be physically owned by anyone. When we go to the theatre or ballet, all that we can carry home is the concept and experience, and this, of course, can be a lasting experience. Christo is interested in the mysterious potential of the concealed object— until its actuality is exposed, our imaginations have free reign. The rocky cliffs of Little Bay push out against the covering, becoming transformed into an entirely new sensation.

Many artists today are more interested in the concept (conceptual art) than in making a permanent mark which will hold the idea for all time. The Amsterdam Arts Council and The Street Foundation jointly financed a series of conceptual, environmental works. One concept was a giant air-inflated tetrahedron made of transparent PVC skin in which a person inside can walk on water by revolving the balloon as he goes. It was made for a walk from England to France.

However, other artists are still concerned with the making of an object that will hold the concept and give it a permanent life.

Margaret Dodd from Adelaide works in ceramic. Like the American Pop artists she uses the ordinary and everyday objects of contemporary life as her subject.

Margaret Dodd (Australian). *On Top of Old Faithful.* Ceramic. Kelvin Grove Teacher's College, Brisbane.

Christo (American, *b.* 1935). *Wrapped Coast, Little Bay,* 1969. Photograph by Shunk-Kender, from an edition of ten, 101.5 x 127 cms. Sydney, The Art Gallery of New South Wales, Anonymous Purchase Fund.

*Camel.* Chinese, T'ang dynasty (7th–10th centuries A.D.). London, The British Museum.

The Chinese artist of the T'ang dynasty uses the camel, which was then the common means of transport—Margaret Dodd uses the Holden car. Notice that in each case the nature of clay and the behaviour of glazes plays an important role in the conception of the object. The T'ang *Camel* has cream, green and yellow glazes which have been allowed to run and merge over a white body.

The modern Italian sculptor, Manzù, has stood at some distance from most modern movements. This bronze of a young girl on a chair has a simple grace—while being very close to actual reality, the subtle simplification of the forms gives the work an arresting monumental dignity.

Giacomo Manzù (Italian, *b.* 1908). *Seated Girl,* Bronze. 114.3 cms high. Ottowa, The National Gallery of Canada.

133

Marisol (American, *b.* Paris, 1930). *Women and Dog,* 1964. Wood, plaster, synthetic polymer paint and miscellaneous items, 182.9 x 208.3 x 40.6 cms. Gift of the Friends of The Whitney Museum, Collection of The Whitney Museum of American Art.

The Venezuelan-American sculptor, Marisol (she uses only her first name) works on a different sort of reality to Manzù. These life-size figures are a comment (not without slight criticism) of chic New York life in the 1960s. Although the figures are carved from wood, Marisol uses an assemblage of real clothes, plaster masks of her own face, and the stuffed dog's head, in order to add impact to the work. Notice how the multiple faces give a feeling of quick darting movement as if the women are walking down a busy street and trying to look all ways at once. In contrast to the two on the outside, the woman in the centre is still and withdrawn, hiding behind a protective outer shell. Like Segal, Marisol does not stand her figures on a base, but has them walking across the gallery floor.

In this section we have seen that structure and form are the servants of man's ideas. In other words, he builds the shape that 'feeds back' to him the essence of his thoughts and attitudes. The great things that man has made, both now and in the past, have the ability to make us (the audience) stop and *think*. In this way they have the ability to widen our perceptions and extend our attitudes. It does not matter if the vehicle of this stimulus is a great monumental stone carving from the past or a transparent plastic bubble —providing it has the power to take hold of our imagination and help us to think with new vitality.

# SECTION THREE

# SURFACE AND MOVEMENT

Artists of this century have so widened the scope of a work of art that we no longer think of art as confined to the art gallery or the 'art object'. We have seen that a 'happening' or situation could extend our awareness and stimulate our thinking and imagination as effectively as any object could. If the artist uses some physical object, such as a painting, a sculptured form, or an architectural form, as the vehicle for transmitting his ideas and attitudes, then the major elements of that work will very likely be *structure, form,* and *space*. However, the nature of that structure can be extended, and invested with added life by the manipulation of the surface or by the use of movement (either actual movement or suggested movement).

The desire to embellish and enliven a surface with line and colour is perhaps one of the earliest creative gestures of man.

For the tribal dance this Mekeo man from the Papuan coast has decorated his face with distinctive tribal markings. This serves both as a communication of his role as ritual dancer of a particular tribe, and also makes the dancer's face an extension of the elaborate headdress and neck ornaments. Today's fashion in make-up may have a very different end result, but the motivation is similar (that is, to attract attention, and to relate the face to the clothes, by matching colours).

Costume and facial decoration of a Mekeo dancer from the Papuan coast near Port Moresby.

Traditionally, each village clan had its own specific headdress, and the many variations on a basic design led to complex structures of feathers (Bird of Paradise plumes) and wood.

Try to imagine the mask without the incised lines which cut across the surface. Without those lines the surface areas would lose their energy and become bland and static. The direction of the incised lines moves your eye across the surface, in a similar way to the painted planes of a cubist picture (see Picasso's *The Bull-Fight Fan,* page 52). The effect of the conflicting lines marking out the surface of the mask would be particularly impressive when seen in the motion of the ritual dance.

In this small gouache by Paul Klee, a simple flat surface becomes enlivened by lines, but in this case the lines express, not the form of the face, but the spirit of the face. If you have ever watched a small child drawing, and listened to the commentary that often accompanies the act, you will have realized that the child is so involved with the act of making that the line is not so much *depicting* the object as *becoming* the object. Paul Klee manages to retain this element of active life in the quality of his

Paul Klee (Swiss, 1879–1940). *Child Consecrated to Suffering,* 1935. Gouache on paper, 15.2 x 23.4 cms. Albright-Knox Art Gallery, Buffalo, Room of Contemporary Art.

A Songe mask (Kifwebe) from Zaïre (formerly Congo). Wood and paint, 11.6 cms high. Courtesy of The Museum of Primitive Art, New York.

The wooden mask from the Congo region was made to be worn during the ritual tribal dances. The holes at the base of the mask originally held long strands of raffia which served to obscure the dancer's body, and so increase the illusion of the spirit 'come to life'. Like the makers of Byzantine icons, the aim of this artist was not to copy nature, but to create a forceful sign which will symbolize the life of the spirit—investing the spirit, not with frail human qualities, but with a dynamic life force of its own.

136

line. Of course, the end result has a control and force that does not exist in the work of small children. Notice the lines that make the eye lids; the upward tilt of the right lid, giving the face its poignant, whimsical quality, as if suffering has been accepted, and also the hard bitter core of anxiety marked out by the W and the dot between the brows.

The black lines of this painting by English artist Bridget Riley convert the flat surface of the canvas to an optical sensation of sharp forward and back movement. The optical effect is so complete that this type of painting has been called *Op* art. The difference between the use of line here and the use of line on the African mask is that in the case of the mask, the lines extend the symbolism of the object, but in this case, the picture is nothing but its own aggressive self—it exists as an object in its own right, without needing any reference to other things.

If we allow our eyes to scan across the surface of this Japanese woodcut from right to left, we become conscious of a series of lyrical movements interrupted by stops or intervals of space, a sensation similar to the experience of listening to music.

Notice how the artist creates this poetic mood of loneliness—this silent stillness which has been disturbed by one ripple of movement, by one breath of wind which shuffles through the lengths of drying cloth. He uses a play of dense opaque areas of colour against open transparent areas, together with the use of a totally sensitive and communicative line.

Bridget Riley (English, *b.* 1931). *Opening.* Oil on canvas, 101.9 x 101.6 cms. Melbourne, The National Gallery of Victoria, Felton Bequest, 1967.

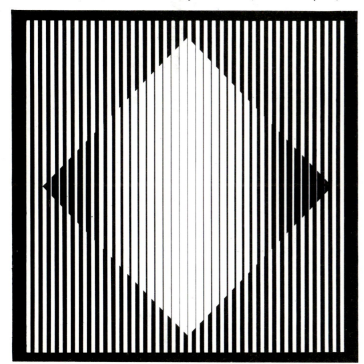

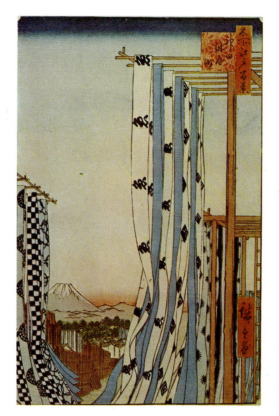

Ichiryusai Hiroshige (Japanese, 1796–1858). *Cloth Dyer's Racks on the High Road, Kanda.* No. 75 of 'The Hundred Views of Yedo, Famous Places'. Adelaide, The Art Gallery of South Australia.

137

This woodcut was made by Hiroshige, a nineteenth century Japanese artist, who was absorbed in portraying the beauty and poetry of the Japanese landscape, endeavouring to recapture in his drawing something of the quality of the great seventeenth century Japanese poet Bashō (Bashō composed *haiku* on nature and the experience of journeys).

As well as landscapes, Hiroshige also made some *kashō* (drawings of flowers and birds). In one: *Kingfisher and Hydrangea,* he manages to sum up the whole world of nature in one bird, one branch, and one flower. The haiku poem which accompanies this particular kashō also aims at expressing a multiplicity of ideas and sensations in a most economic and minimal way. It reads:

> The hydrangea
> Does not grow in water
> But it seems to smell of water.

*Shiva as Nataraja* (Shiva as Lord of the Dancers). Southern India, *c.* 1800. Copper. Courtesy, Museum of Fine Arts, Boston, Marianne Brimmer Fund.

Most works of art fall roughly into three categories: the objective approach in which detail is depicted with minute care and accuracy; the opposite, that is, a subjective approach with disregard for outer appearances; and thirdly, a combination of these two, which is an attempt to discover oneself in the object—to identify with it. The work of Hiroshige falls into this last category.

This copper figure from India shows the god **Shiva as Lord of Dancers.** The eighteenth century Indian artist who modelled this figure and later cast it in copper was trying to suggest a movement that never ends—the dance that goes on for ever. In this case it is not the lines of the surface that suggest the movement but the swing and turn of multiple shapes. The four arms represent the four aspects of the god's nature; you will notice in one hand a small drum, this represents the very first sound of creation; in the opposite hand a flame symbolizes destruction, a third hand is upraised in a protective gesture, while the fourth points to a small figure at Shiva's feet who signifies evil, overcome by the spirit of the dance. Notice how the flamelike shape behind Shiva's head radiates out like the rays of the halo in Christian symbolism, to suggest the god's supernatural power.

The twentieth century American sculptor, Alexander Calder, makes use of actual movement. These sculptures, called *mobiles,* are so finely balanced that the slightest movement of air causes the structure to swing so that the shapes inter-change their positions, marking out a prescribed area of space. Whereas the shapes of the Indian statue suggest a backwards and forwards swing of movement, in this case the movement becomes actual.

The fascination of movement can be introduced in city environments with the imaginative use of water. In the cement and asphalt world of a large city, the sight and sound of water can immediately refresh us. Even in the captive and confined pools and fountains of city squares we can be reminded of waterfalls and running creeks (in much the same way as a caged animal in a zoo can remind us of the wild freedom in its natural state). New pumping

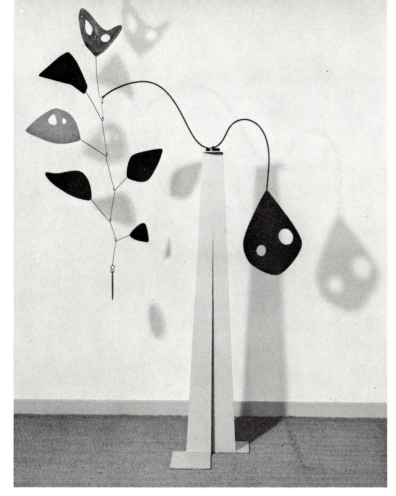

Alexander Calder (American, *b.* 1898). *Bird in Tree,* 1949. Standing mobile. Moderna Museet, Stockholm.

A decorated Gothic cathedral — the facade of Wells Cathedral in England. Built 1180–*c.* 1425.

Just as sculptors manipulate the surface of their works to give added life or tension, so the surface of a building can add to the life of the structure. You can see how sculpture adds life and movement to the facades of the Gothic cathedral and the Hindu temple. They both seem to grow up like some complicated cellular structure in nature, wherein each part has its own life, but together the parts become a unified whole.

systems have made it possible for water to be used extensively in city areas. In the past lavish water displays were paid for dearly. Louis XIV of France assigned 3000 Swiss mercenaries to dig the canals to supply the networks of fountains in the Versailles gardens. The task took two years and many lives—almost half of the original 3000 died in the process—and the fountains could still only be turned on for special occasions!

One of the five gateways into the Menashi Temple at Madurai, in the Indian state of Madras.

139

A close-up view of the carving on the Hindu temple gateway.

Joern Utzon (Danish, *b.* 1918). The Sydney Opera House. Pre-cast concrete faced with ceramic tiles.

Carved statuary on one of the doorways of Chartres Cathedral in France. 1194–1260.

The surface of the Sydney Opera House does not rely on the complicated activities of the surface, but more on the sculptured thrust of the sails against the taut smoothness of the white ceramic tiles that seem to be holding the energy in. Do you notice a similar feeling in Henry Moore's *Two Piece No. 11?* The large full shapes seem to be pushing up against the smoothed surface. Just as there are elements of the architectural in Moore's *Two Piece,* so there are elements of the sculptural in Utzon's Opera House.

After looking at the things that man has made, both now and in the past, you have probably realized that a work of art does not rely only on the degree of skill that has gone into its making,

Henry Moore (English, *b.* 1898). Maquette for *Two Piece No. II.* Plaster for bronze, 10.2 cms long.

but more on the degree of life and force that the image holds. The skilled stonemasons who worked on Michelangelo's statues would have been at a loss if confronted by an untouched block of marble, with no great mind to direct them. Nor does a work of art rely on subject matter: the artist selects from his environment that which is significant to him, and then presents it in such a way that it may become significant to many people.

However, although the work of art may not rely entirely on skill or subject matter, it does rely on you, because its active life lies in its ability to influence your thoughts and sensibilities.

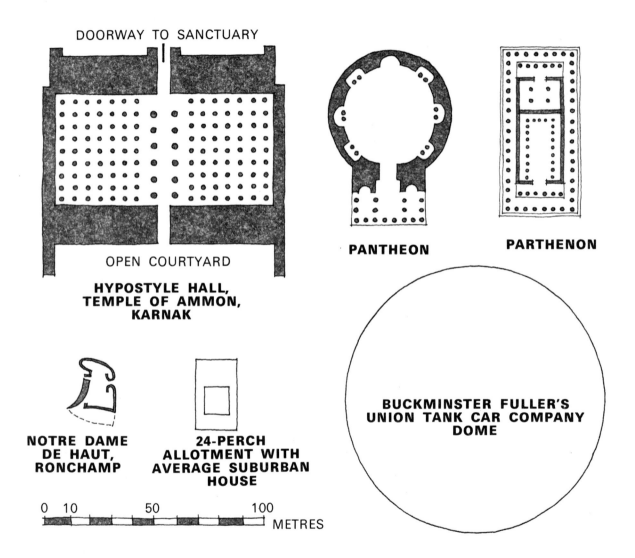

DOORWAY TO SANCTUARY

OPEN COURTYARD

**HYPOSTYLE HALL,
TEMPLE OF AMMON,
KARNAK**

**PANTHEON**

**PARTHENON**

**NOTRE DAME
DE HAUT,
RONCHAMP**

**24-PERCH
ALLOTMENT WITH
AVERAGE SUBURBAN
HOUSE**

**BUCKMINSTER FULLER'S
UNION TANK CAR COMPANY
DOME**

0  10       50          100
METRES

# EXERCISES

## EXERCISES IN THE USE OF SPACE

We have discussed the two possibilities of the use of space in pictures—the illusion of space going 'in', as in van Eyck's *The Marriage of Jan Arnolfini and his Wife;* and the use of space that goes 'across', that is, the interval between shapes across a surface as in the early Egyptian frieze painting *Singers and Dancers at a Banquet* on page 38.

We can interpret these six circles in two ways—they can be circles of the same size and tone disappearing into the distance, becoming smaller and lighter in tone as they move back in space. Or they could be six circles of different sizes and tones sitting flat on the picture plane. If we want them to sit flat on the same plane we have to become conscious of the interval between the circles, and to feel the stretch of space between each shape pulling across the surface.

If you try some experiments in which you use these two different sensations of space, you will make discoveries which you can apply to your own work.

We will start with creating a sensation of three dimensional space. Paint four sheets of paper with four distinct tones, ranging from black to a light grey (use a sponge roller if you have one). Then cut each sheet into circles ranging in size from large to small, the largest being about the size of a 20 cent piece. Place one of these circles on a large sheet of blank paper. Notice how this first mark immediately sets up a two dimensional space relationship with the edges of the paper, making the space around it significant. Now add another circle. If this is a different size and tone, a three dimensional space will start to form, together with the two dimensional space which exists between each mark you make.

Now start experimenting with more additions. See what happens when a close density of circles forms, as opposed to open areas. Try a close density of small light-toned shapes against an area of open dark-toned shapes. After each addition notice the sensation of space that you have produced and try to decide why the space works in this way. When you have experimented with many different possibilities, you could stick the circles down onto the paper.

We will use a similar method to find out something about the properties of two dimensional space. This time we could use a method of subtraction rather than addition. Cut out enough identical black circles to completely cover a sheet of paper. Remove one circle and notice how significant this interval becomes. Remove a vertical row of circles and then a horizontal row. Again, each time you make a subtraction notice how the 'negative' spaces begin to play a positive role in the structure of the surface.

After doing this exercise, you could make some drawings of the negative spaces between objects in the room, or between trees and houses outside.

Try a similar exercise using different textures and different colours. In order to discover the space properties of colour, you could paint several strips of paper with different colours (again, it is easier to get clear colours if you use a roller)—a clear red, a yellow, and a clear blue. Paint another sheet of paper a neutral grey. Cut the grey sheet and the coloured strips into small squares or circles and cover a sheet of white paper with the grey shapes. Now remove one grey shape from anywhere on the sheet and substitute a coloured shape. Does this colour set up a space relation with the grey? Keep substituting coloured shapes with the grey ones, and each time see if the colour has sufficient 'bounce' or energy to produce a sensation of floating forward from the background of grey, and if some of the colours have more forward bounce than others.

After completing this exercise you could make further experiments with colour. See how many different colours you can make

from the three primary colours (red, yellow, blue). You can use black and white in order to obtain pale tints of a colour or greyed down versions of a colour. Set each colour side by side on a sheet of paper, and when you find no further possibilities, study the sheet in order to decide how the energy of each colour works in relation to the other colours on the sheet.

So far we have been dealing with an *illusion* of space, that is discovering different means of evoking a sensation of space on a flat surface. However, we must also consider actual spaces; spaces which we can move in and measure. You could start by considering the space of your own allotments, noticing how the available space is being used, could some spaces become more significant and interesting by enclosure? Could some areas be opened up, or could an open area be made more interesting by punctuating the space with trees? Look with fresh eyes, which are not too conditioned by preconceived ideas of what a suburban garden should look like. You could make a small model which redesigns the lay-out of your allotment, or some particular part of it, concentrating on making the space more pleasant for people to use.

Visit some part of your city or town, preferably an area which you feel could be improved. Look at this area as a space enclosed by surrounding buildings. Then consider the people who are going to use this space, remembering that the human element is most important. Now redesign the area, by making either a small model or a drawing. Before you start, try to imagine you have been walking in the city streets all day, and what it is you would like to find on walking into this particular area.

After using space yourself, you can look with new interest at the many different ways people have used space both in the past and now.

Look for other examples not illustrated in this book, of the use of space in works of art. See if you can decide why the space has been used, and how the sensation of space has been achieved.

Some works will interest you more than others. Find out more about the artists who produced these works, looking for as many other examples of their work as possible.

You could compile your own list of works of art which have made significant use of space, using some examples from this book, but adding others of your own.

## EXERCISES IN THE USE OF STRUCTURE

Our concept of structure derives from forms in the natural world. As we have no other concept of form and structure, we tend to relate the things we make to the natural order of things in the world around us. The size of the hypostyle hall of the Egyptian temple is impressive because of its relation to the size of man. The golden proportion used by the Greeks is a proportion found again and again in the natural world. The golden mean rectangle which the Greeks used as a basis for the Parthenon is a rectangle with

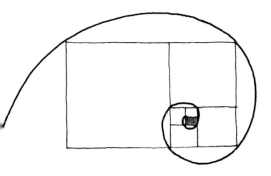

The shaded golden mean rectangle has had square 1 added, making another golden mean rectangle, to which square 2 has been added, and so on.

a number of peculiarities. For instance, by building a square onto the longest side of the rectangle, you produce another larger golden mean rectangle, and so it can go on. If you construct a number of golden mean rectangles in this way, and connect the corners of all the rectangles with a curved line, a spiral results, which is one of the most persistent growth forms in nature.

You can construct a golden mean rectangle by starting with a square ABCD. Bisect the square with a line EF. With the point of a compass on F and radius FA drop an arc to cut CB extended.

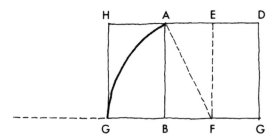

Constructing a golden mean rectangle.

This point will give you the position of the side GH which produces the golden mean rectangle HGCD. Because of the pecularities of this rectangle, HGBA is also a golden mean rectangle. As you can see, you could keep diminishing and extending this rectangle indefinitely. Like a cellular growth in nature, each addition maintains the same basic structure and proportion.

Just as the Greeks looked to the natural world to discover their concept of a perfect structural proportion, we could start by looking at some natural structures. Many things in nature are supported by an internal structure—a skeleton structure. Look at a tree, noticing how the leaves are supported on a complex skeleton of trunk, branches, and twigs. Make some simple diagrams of several tree structures using a brush and ink or black paint. Think of the lines as a diagram describing the way the tree functions structurally. Notice how the tree, like a person, starts with a strong central trunk (the backbone) which branches out into smaller divisions which in turn divide into the numerous twigs, which hold the leaves (just as our limbs become fingers and toes).

Look at other objects, both natural and man-made forms, and make diagrammatic drawings explaining their structure.

Perhaps you could use one of these drawings as the basis of a three dimensional structure, using pliable wire, or balsa wood strips. If you use balsa wood, use a quick drying cement and support each strut while the cement dries. When you have finished, mount the sculpture onto a base. While you were making these drawings and the piece of sculpture, you probably noticed the way each part relies on and relates to the next part—the many parts together becoming the total structure.

So far, we have been looking at existing structures in the world around us; now I want you to consider the visual structuring of a painting or drawing. A painter is faced with a blank surface on which he has to structure his vision or ideas in such a way that the idea communicates its own life and energy. Just as in nature there are many varieties of structure—the firm, clearly articulated structure of a pine tree, the dynamic structure of running water, the loosely held structure of a cloud—so in a work of art there are many alternatives. An artist may use a geometric structure of mass and line as seen in the work of Piero della Francesca, or a structure of colour as seen in a Cézanne painting, or he may use the actual paint to produce the structural energy of the work, as seen in a Jackson Pollock.

We have already described structure as the way in which an object or complex holds itself together—in a work of art it is the way in which the parts together become a whole. As you look about you, you see multiple shapes which your mind sorts into a single image. In order to do this the eye selects major structural lines, masses, or sensations, the smaller details becoming apparent only when we focus on them, and then we lose the concept of the total image.

Just as you made a diagram of the structure of a tree, make some diagrammatic drawings of the manner in which your eye and mind structures your vision. To do this use a brush and ink, or charcoal, and before you start concentrate on the total image —we will suppose it is a view out the window. As you look, your eye will be registering the major shapes, directions, and masses. Now close your eyes for a minute and see what your visual memory has recorded. This will give you an indication of the major lines and masses on which to build your structure. Make a very simple diagram of what you see—for instance the leafy structure of a near tree could become a broken area of dots seen against the solid mass of a building in the distance, the curve of a branch may relate to the vertical of a telegraph pole. Think of each part as being a part of a whole, noticing how your eye is constantly relating one shape to another in order to register the total image. After making a diagrammatic sketch in ink you may want to build a more complex structure using colour, texture, etc., or you may feel you can simplify the structure further in order to arrive at the essence of what you see.

Just as an architect starts by building the main structural supports, which will later hold the details, so your first drawing should be the skeleton structure that could hold the many parts and details together. Try not to draw each object in detail methodically before you move on to the next, but allow your hand to respond spontaneously to the way your eye moves from part to part, picking up a line here, a mass there, a broken area against a solid one, etc.

Look again at the reproductions in this book and make sure you can understand the means whereby the artists have structured their works. Again, look for other examples not used in this book.

Compile your own list of paintings and the artists who produced them, dividing the list into four sections:

1. Structures which are built on a geometry of mass and line.
2. Structures which are built on the vitality of the brush stroke (look at the work of Vincent van Gogh).
3. Structures which are built on the vitality of colour.
4. Structures which seem to defy any classification, yet hold together because of a sense of rightness which cannot be adequately explained.

Of course, most works are a combination of these things, but you can often detect a major structure which holds the picture together.

Compile a list of three dimensional works, dividing your list into 1, sculptors who have structured their works on mass and surface tension, and 2, sculptors who have used an environment or situation to clarify an idea.

## EXERCISES IN THE USE OF SURFACE AND MOVEMENT

Painters often use colour to create a movement across the surface of their pictures, or a repetition of certain colours which cause the eyes to move from point to point. Look at some pictures from this point of view; you could try to find a reproduction of Pieter Brueghel's *Wedding Dance* (Brueghel was a sixteenth century Flemish painter) and notice the way the shapes of red dance across the surface simulating the bouncing movement of the dance.

We will see if we can convert a static situation into one of movement with the use of colour. Cut thin strips (about 6 millimetres wide) from a sheet of grey paper and stick them down on a sheet of white paper forming a grid of 24 mm squares. We will try to create a sensation of movement on the surface by changing some of the grey lines to coloured lines. Suppose you paint over a short length of one of the grey lines with a vivid orange-red, or a pale blue—you will notice that the addition of colour immediately brings in a new activity. Start building with colour onto different sections of the grey grid, concentrating on producing some sense of movement. You could try to direct the movement into the centre of the grid or out to the edges, or to make the whole area vibrate with movement.

Paint a picture of an old lady walking down the street and a young man walking quickly past. Describe these two movements in terms of colour, by using short vertical or diagonal strokes of paint. Make the colour of the old lady move slowly and evenly across the page as she carefully puts one foot in front of the other. Change the colour to indicate the slow rhythm of her walk. Now make the young man swing quickly past, springing lightly from one foot to the other. Again change the colour to indicate the bounce of rhythm as he moves.

You could think of other situations of movement which could be interpreted in terms of colour. You will notice that the eye picks up movement of colour, in much the same way as the ear picks up rhythm of sound in music.

Try the same thing with textures. You could take rubbings of many different surfaces, then organize them on a page so that some sensation of movement is produced; or you could build an assemblage of textured shapes. In each case try to control the way the eye moves across the surface by the use of colour, line, shape or texture.

Build a relief with projecting parts which will catch the light and cast shadows. You could use clay for this, or assemble found objects, or even cut flaps from a sheet of paper—the flaps can then be bent back so that they project and catch the light. You will remember that the ancient Greeks considered this aspect of sculpture (light) in carving the friezes of the Parthenon—making use of cast shadows on the external frieze which received direct sunlight. The Australian sculptor Clive Murray White also makes use of light in order to create the strange optical effect of his three discs (page 81).

When you have finished your relief, try various lightings, noticing how the light and cast shadows can affect the form.

You could try to produce a sensation of movement or changing plane by manipulating lines, tones, or dots on a flat surface. Make several small experiments first and then select the most successful to carry out on a larger scale. If you use lines or dots, you could cut them from black paper and stick them down to the surface.

Make a study of different natural surfaces—a mossy rock, a spotted leaf, a cracked pavement, sand, a butterfly's wing, etc. You could either draw or make a photographic record of them. Make another collection of interesting man-made surfaces—a wicker basket, a woven rug, the facade of a building, a patterned fabric, a patterned tea cup, etc.

Once you start looking at the many ways nature and man embellish the surface of a form, you will probably notice that nature is invariably successful, and that man's failures arise from a failure to relate the surface to the form, or a failure to create any real interest or vitality of shape, line, or colour. Try to find some photographs of Greek vases and notice how the artists have embellished the surface with decorations which play an important role in the vitality and character of the vase. Can you find any modern pieces of pottery in which the surface involvement plays an equally important role?

# INDEX

# GLOSSARY

**Abacus:** A flat stone slab forming the top part of a capital.

**Abstract Art:** Non-representational art, i.e., painting without subject which relies entirely on the activity of form, space, and colour.

**Academic Art:** The art perpetuated by the established academies, which continue to reproduce a form of art which has already resolved itself and fulfilled its aims — a non-experimental art.

**Action Painting:** A form of abstract expressionism in which the artist allows the paint to become the vehicle of expression. The marks made by the paint as it is splashed, dragged, or dribbled across the canvas is directed by the subconscious, intuitive instincts of the artist, as well as by the painting itself as certain forms and energies begin to emerge. 113.

**Aisle:** Side section of a church which lies parallel to the nave and allows free passage from entrance to altar. 20.

**Apse:** Semicircular or multi-angular recess at the rear of a church or cathedral. 19, 20, 98.

**Arcade:** A series of arches supported on a row of columns. 18, 20.

**Art Nouveau** (AHR noo-VOH): (French, new art) This emerged in the 1890s and was a conscious attempt to combat the dehumanizing elements of industrialization by encouraging personal expression through handcrafts, and by formulating a new decorative style based on nature. The curved tendril, the vine leaf, the peacock feather, the lily, etc., were converted into sinuous linear designs which were used in architectural features, fabric design, pottery and glass design, and furniture. 101.

**Baroque** (bah-ROK): Art and architecture of the period approximately 1600 to 1750. All the arts were enlisted and acted in concert, making a theatrical and emotional assault on the spectator. Painting was highly illusionistic and sculptors made full use of the play of light on surface and contour. 74.

**Barrel Vault:** A semicircular ceiling of stone, brick, or cement. 23.

**Basilica:** A rectangular building divided into a central nave and side aisles. Used by the Romans as law courts and the early Christians as churches. 98.

**Blind Arcade:** A row of columns with connecting arches built against a wall as a decorative feature.

**Broken Colour:** In order to avoid loss of brilliance by mixing, secondary and tertiary are produced by placing small strokes of primary colours side by side; e.g., yellow placed beside blue will produce a sensation of green from a certain distance.

**Buttress:** A mass of masonry built to resist the outward thrust of a wall which is carrying the weight of a heavy superstructure.

**Cantilever:** A structural weight-carrying member which projects from a building and is made secure, not by support from below, but by the weight of the building on the fixed end. 102, 103.

**Cathedral:** (Greek *cathedra*, seat or throne) Literally, the Bishop's seat, hence, the Bishops' own churches.

**Cella** (SELL-ah): The chief apartment of a temple, where the image of a god stood. 16, 72, 94.

**Chiaroscuro** (kyaroh-SKOOroh): (Italian, light-dark) Creating an illusion of volume by using a shaded area, thus suggesting that the form is round and turning away from the light. Also applied to the organization of dark areas and light areas in a pictorial composition, creating a similar sensation of movement forward into the light and back into the shadows. 53.

**c.:** Latin *circa*, which means *about;* e.g., *c.* 600 B.C.

**Classic art:** Pertaining to ancient Greek art, and applied to the attainment of an order and harmony which comes close to perfection.

**Classicism:** Refers to that which strives towards the excellence of the antique classic style.

**Clerestory** (or clearstorey): Windows which allow light and air into the central part of a building which would otherwise be cut off from the outside. The central part of the building is raised clear of the main roof level, with the clerestory windows in the wall between the two roof levels. 15, 92, 98.

**Cloister:** Covered walk around an open square, connecting the church to other parts of the monastery.

**Collage** (koll-ARZH): (French, to stick) A picture built up wholly or partly from pieces of paper, cloth, or other material stuck onto a canvas or other backing. This device was used by the Cubists, and in his last years Matisse used pieces of coloured paper as a complete substitute for painting. 2.

**Colonnade:** A row of columns.

**Column:** A vertical support, usually consisting of a base, shaft, and capital.

**Complementary Colour:** Each primary colour — red, yellow, blue — has a complementary formed by a mixture of the other two, e.g., red and yellow make orange, which is the complement of blue. If used at equal strength or tonal intensity, these complementary colours will intensify each other when placed side by side.

**Contemporary Art:** Work produced in this generation.

**Crypt:** (Greek *kryptos*, hidden) A space entirely or partly under a building — in churches, generally beneath the chancel or choir and used for burial in early times. 20.

**Cubism:** A movement which proposed a new realism based on a knowledge and experience of the physical world as well as its visual aspects. Hence, objects were presented, not as they appear from a fixed viewpoint, but as a total experience of their many aspects combined into one image. 51, 53.

**Curtain-wall:** An exterior wall of modern building which consists of a light metal frame holding glass, and fixed to the structural part of the building. It carries no load and is not part of the structural system. 29.

**Dada:** An attempt to revalue and reassess the modern situation by the destruction of outmoded values. By ridicule, shock tactics, and the unusual, the Dadaists hoped to shake themselves and others from a complacent apathy. 130–132.

**Divisionism:** Divided or broken colour. See Pointillism.

**Drum:** A circular wall which elevates and supports a dome.

**Dynamic:** Pertaining to movement. In painting, a sensation of movement, energy, or animation on the static surface of the canvas.

**Entablature:** The structure immediately above the columns of a Greek temple. It consists of three separate beams — the architrave, the frieze and the cornice. 93.

**Exedra** (pl.*exedrae*): In Greek buildings a recess or alcove with a raised seat where the discussions of learned men took place. The Romans applied the term to any semi-circular or rectangular recess with benches. It is also applied to semicircular apse or niche in a church.

**Expressionism:** An art form which reveals the artist's inner emotions and feelings. Sometimes the artist distorts and exaggerates in order to increase the emotional impact of the picture.

**Flying Buttress:** An arched support which springs from the buttressed outside wall of a Gothic church and spans the aisle roof to support the wall of the nave. 100.

**Free Standing Sculpture:** Sculpture standing in space so that it can be viewed from all sides.

**Fresco:** (Italian, fresh) Powder pigment mixed with water only and applied to freshly laid plaster. The pigment is absorbed into the surface of the wall and so becomes a permanent part of the wall.

**Frieze:** A long strip of decoration near the top of a wall, either painted or carved in relief. 72.

**Genre** (zharnr): Realistic representation of domestic and rustic scenes taken from everyday life.

**Gouache** (gwarsh): Watercolour made thick and opaque with white paint. 136–137.

**Graphic art:** Based on drawing and line as opposed to painting. Also applied to all printing methods — etching, lithography, engraving, etc.

**Hypostyle Hall:** A hall where the roof is supported on numerous pillars. 15, 16, 92.

**Icon:** (Greek *ikon*, image) A portable painted or modelled image of a holy subject, used by the Russian and Greek Orthodox churches. These images were simplified in order to become easily recognized forms with the power of instant communication. 42, 136.

**Iconography:** Pictorial representations to which a particular meaning can be attached, e.g., the lamb in Christian iconography, or the bamboo in Chinese iconography (which signifies the Confucian ideal of a man who bends to outside influences or forces,

but never breaks or loses his integrity).

**Illusionism:** The virtuoso use of pictorial techniques such as perspective and chiaroscuro in order to deceive the eye into believing that which is painted to be that which is real.

**Impressionism:** The first of the modern movements. A nineteenth century style in painting concerned with portraying the real quality of light in terms of colour energy. Light, which manifests itself in colour, becomes the principle subject of the composition. 116.

**Intensity of colour:** The brilliance of a colour.

**Lintel:** The horizontal beam over an opening.

**Local colour:** The actual colour of an object; e.g., a lemon is yellow.

**Maquette** (mah-KET): (French, small model) A small-scale model or sketch in clay, wax, etc., for a larger sculpture. 82.

**Medium:** The means or materials (such as oil paint, clay, or marble) used by the artist to express his ideas. Also the liquid vehicle used for mixing pigments (oil, water, egg).

**Minaret:** The tall tower usually attached to a mosque from which the faithful are called to prayer.

**Mobile:** A sculpture composed of suspended or balanced forms which swing or revolve. The movement is activated either by air currents or by motor. 4, 78, 138–139.

**Monochrome:** Different tones of the one colour.

**Mosaic:** A surface decoration composed of small blocks of coloured glass, stone, or marble, set in a cement or plaster bed. Often used as a wall decoration or a floor surface. 18, 20.

**Mosque:** A Mohammedan place of worship.

**Motif** (moh-TEEF): The subject or idea used by the artist.

**Mural:** Decoration on a wall surface, by painting, relief sculpture, or mosaic.

**Nave:** The main central part of a church designed to house the congregation. 19, 20, 22, 98.

**Niche:** A hollowed recess in a wall for a statue or ornament.

**Non-Objective art:** That which makes no attempt to represent objects or nature — abstract art.

**Oil paint:** Pigment mixed with linseed, poppy, or walnut oil.

**Order:** Signifies a column together with the entablature above. Greek architects used three styles to determine the decorative form of a building — Doric, Ionic, and Corinthian. 93, 94, 101.

**Pediment:** The enclosed triangular section at the end of the pitched roof of a Greek temple.

**Pendentive:** The triangular area of masonry wedged between the weight-carrying arches which support a dome above a square compartment. 97.

**Perspective:** A mathematical system for representing forms in space on a flat surface. The basic assumption of the system is that although parallel lines never meet, they appear to do so if moving away from the eye of the spectator; e.g., the parallel sides of a long straight road which appear to converge to a point on the eye level of the spectator. This system was probably formulated by Brunelleschi in the early fifteenth century.

**Pier:** A supporting mass of masonry, more massive than a column.

**Pilaster:** A decorative column attached to a wall and carrying no weight.

**Plastic, Plasticity:** (Greek *plasso*, mould) Giving shape to formless yielding material such as wax, clay, or paint. 68.

**Pointillism:** The scientific and precise placing together of dots of colour in order to maintain the brilliance of a colour sensation. 116.

**Portico:** A colonnaded entrance or vestibule.

**Post and Lintel:** A horizontal beam upheld on two vertical supports. Also called trabeated style. 92.

**Primary Colours:** In paint — red, yellow, blue. In theory, any colour can be made by the mixing of these three colours (with the addition of black and white).

**Renaissance:** (REN-ay-sans): The revival of art and learning under the influence of rediscovered Classical models.

The new thinking invested man and his works with a new dignity and importance. In the early Renaissance there was a great fidelity to nature which in the High Renaissance became secondary to the concept of perfect form.

**Salon:** During the seventeenth century exhibitions by members of the French Royal Academy were held in the Salon d'Apollon in the Louvre — hence the name. After the Revolution the exhibitions were held annually. The selection committee obtained a stranglehold on French painting, as there were no other public exhibitions of any standing, and these men held the power to exclude any painter of whom they did not approve.

**School of Painting:** Indicating a relationship which exists between painters as a result of 1, the artists belonging to a similar culture or district, or 2, artists sharing similar thoughts or attitudes; e.g., School of Florence, Impressionist School.

**Secondary Colour:** A mixture of any two primary colours, thus orange (red and yellow), purple (red and blue), and green (blue and yellow).

**Stylized Art:** This occurs when an art form becomes removed from its origins in nature, and is based on a previous representation — thus becoming a style. This repetition of an art form generally results in a simplification which concentrates on the essential elements of the shape (e.g., Byzantine and Egyptian painting).

**Stylobate:** In Greek architecture the upper step forming a platform on which a colonnade is placed. Collectively the three steps of a Greek Doric temple constitute a crepidoma.

**Symbolic:** In art, the use of forms or shapes which convey a message by means of associated ideas, e.g., the blue robe of the Virgin symbolizing purity; the golden halo symbolizing purity of spirit.

**Symmetry:** Perfect balance of weight on either side of a central axis.

**Tactile:** A sense of touch, either actual or evoked by suggestion.

**Technique:** The manner in which an artist works with materials and tools.

**Tempera:** Pigment mixed with a binder in order to hold it to a surface (tempered). It can be applied to a gesso (plaster and glue, or whiting and glue) coated wooden panel or canvas stretched on wood. Egg tempera is pigment mixed with egg yolk. A tempera mixture is water soluble.

**Tertiary Colour:** A mixture of the three primary colours to produce the neutral colours; e.g., orange (red and yellow) with a small part of blue will produce brown.

**Tesserae:** Small cubes of glass, ceramic, marble or stone which are used to make mosaics.

**Texture:** The character or nature of a surface.

**Tone:** The different strengths or values which exist on a scale between black and white. Can apply to the degree of lightness or darkness of any colour.

**Trabeated Style:** (Latin *trabs*, a beam) See post and lintel.

**Tracery:** The ornamental carving cut into the stone directly above a group of Gothic windows and below the pointed arch which surrounds and unites the group. This fretted stone enlarged the window area allowing more light into the cathedral.

**Traditional:** The established style or method handed down from the past.

**Transept:** Portion of a cathedral at right angle to the nave. 1.

**Triforium:** The open gallery immediately above the nave arcade of a large church and below the clerestory windows. It backed onto the sloping roof over the aisle. Sometimes this section was only a false gallery, consisting of a blind arcade.

**Value:** See tone.

**Vault:** Arched ceiling of masonry or concrete. 23, 28, 94, 96, 101.

**Vestibule:** An ante-room to a larger apartment of a building. 15.

**Volume:** A three dimensional mass — either of matter or of space; e.g., the volume of a mountain, or the space volume of a room. In painting, volume is implied by the use of colour, line, or chiaroscuro; in sculpture and architecture it is actual.

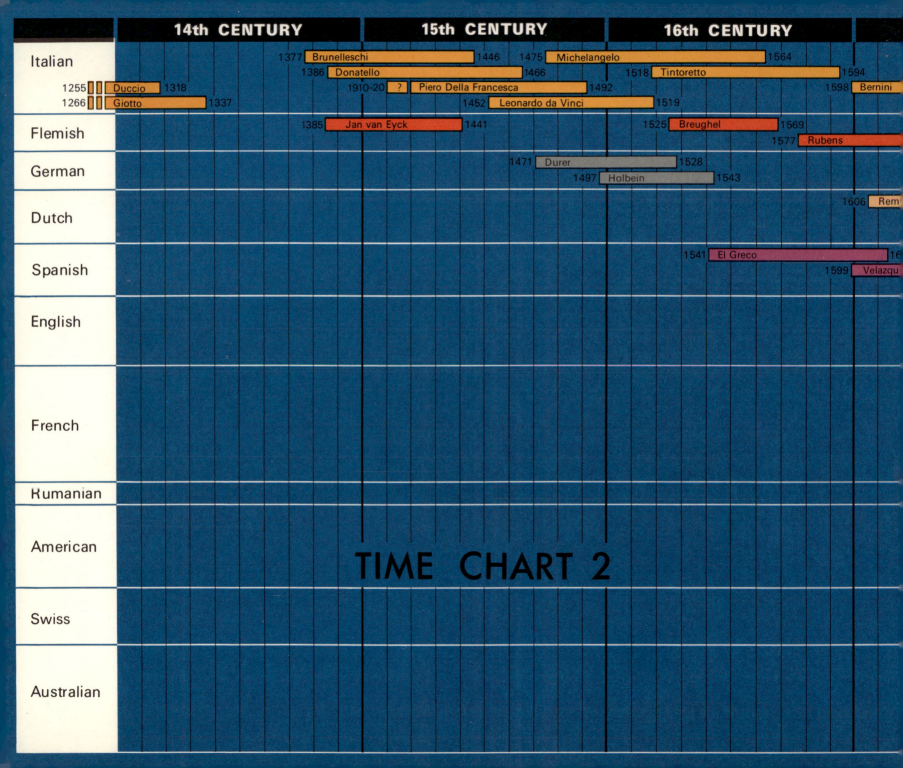

| | 14th CENTURY | 15th CENTURY | 16th CENTURY | |
|---|---|---|---|---|

**Italian**
1377 Brunelleschi 1446 · 1475 Michelangelo 1564
1386 Donatello 1466 · 1518 Tintoretto 1594
1255 Duccio 1318 · 1910-20 ? Piero Della Francesca 1492 · 1598 Bernini
1266 Giotto 1337 · 1452 Leonardo da Vinci 1519

**Flemish**
1385 Jan van Eyck 1441 · 1525 Breughel 1569
1577 Rubens

**German**
1471 Durer 1528
1497 Holbein 1543

**Dutch**
1606 Rem

**Spanish**
1541 El Greco 16
1599 Velazqu

**English**

**French**

**Rumanian**

**American**

TIME CHART 2

**Swiss**

**Australian**